P9-EAJ-782

Some Late Victorian Attitudes

The Ewing Lectures

David Daiches has taught at universities in both Britain and the United States; since 1961 he has been Professor of English at the University of Sussex. He is the author of *Critical Approaches to Literature*, *Milton* and *A Study of Literature for Readers and Critics*, and he is an editor of the distinguished *Norton Anthology of English Literature*.

By the same author

CRITICAL APPROACHES TO LITERATURE
MILTON
A STUDY OF LITERATURE FOR READERS AND CRITICS
NORTON ANTHOLOGY OF ENGLISH LITERATURE (*editor*)

Some Late Victorian Attitudes

The Ewing Lectures
University of California at Los Angeles, 1967

DAVID DAICHES

W · W · NORTON & COMPANY · INC.
NEW YORK

PRINTED IN GREAT BRITAIN

Preface

The three essays that follow constitute the Ewing Lectures delivered at the University of California, Los Angeles, n November 1967. I should like to record my gratitude to tne University of California at Los Angeles for the opportunity afforded me to give these lectures and for the kindness and hospitality shown me on the UCLA campus. I should also like to express my sadness that Professor Ewing, who endowed this annual lectureship, should have been so grievously ill during my brief stay in Los Angeles and should have died within a few days of my leaving.

The subject I chose for these lectures was determined partly by my own long-standing interest in the late Victorian period and partly by a feeling that the doubts, uncertainties, rebellions and sense of alienation from tradition that one finds so widespread in the late nineteenth century might have a special interest and relevance for a generation of American (and for that matter British) students deeply and uneasily aware of the gap between themselves and their elders. The generous reception accorded the lectures by a gratifyingly large audience leads me to believe that my expectation here was correct.

The lectures are here presented exactly as I delivered them, unencumbered with footnotes or detailed citing of sources (all of which are easily discoverable) except for the fuller description of critical works alluded to or quoted from in the text.

University of Sussex DAVID DAICHES

The Ewing Lectures

I

When, in *The Brothers Karamazov*, Ivan expressed the view that without a belief in God and immortality 'everything would be permissible', he was saying very much what Tennyson had said eight years before the publication of Dostoievsky's novel. Discussing immortality with his friend James Thomas Knowles, the architect and editor, and the Irish poet William Allingham in 1872, Tennyson said: 'If I ceased to believe in any chance of another life, and of a great Personality somewhere in the Universe, I should not care a pin for anything.' And in 1850 Charles Kingsley had declared that if God were a deceiver 'I'd go and blow my brains out and be rid of the whole thing at once, I would indeed.' One of the reasons why so many Victorians agonized about the existence of God was that all human values seemed to depend on it. When they were sceptical, they took no joy in their scepticism, as the men of the eighteenth-century Enlightenment had. David Hume's theological doubts did not prevent him either from developing a confident morality or from leading a happy social life. But scepticism was not as a rule a happy frame of mind for Victorians. They tended either to fight their way out of it, as Tennyson did to his own satisfaction in *In Memoriam*, or torture themselves with their own irony, as Clough did –

Is in reason's grave precision,
Nothing more, nothing less,
Than a peculiar conformation,
Constitution, and condition
Of the brain and of the belly?
Is it true, ye gods who cheat us?
And that's the way ye treat us? –

or gloom over the ebb of faith, as Arnold did in *Dover Beach*, or, if they were successful in developing an agnostic ethic, to bring to it, as George Eliot did, all the stern imperatives of Puritan Christianity.

One of the more familiar stories about George Eliot is F. W. H. Myers's reminiscence of her remarks made in 1873 about God, Immortality and Duty. They are worth recalling and setting beside the words of Tennyson already quoted. 'I remember,' wrote Myers, 'how, at Cambridge, I walked with her once in the Fellows' Garden of Trinity, on an evening of rainy May; and she, stirred somewhat beyond her wont, and taking as her text the three words which have been used so often as the inspiring trumpet-calls of men – the words *God*, *Immortality*, *Duty* – pronounced, with terrible earnestness, how inconceivable was the *first*, how unbelievable the *second*, and yet how peremptory and absolute the *third*. Never, perhaps, have sterner accents affirmed the sovereignty of impersonal and unrecompensing Law.'

So if for Tennyson in 1872 disbelief in God and immortality meant that he would 'not care a pin for anything', for George Eliot in 1873 this Karamazov-Tennyson dilemma was resolved. God and immortality were unbelievable, but duty remained paramount. In George Eliot the nonconformist conscience co-existed with scepticism. If this is explicable partly in terms of the evangelical influences on her own early life, it still has wider implications. It points forward to a late Victorian mood of stoicism, of heroic endurance for its own sake, that is more widely represented among men of letters at the end of the nineteenth century than is generally realized. The value lies in the endurance rather than in any moral end that is to be attained by that endurance:

> Out of the night that covers me
>   Black as the Pit from pole to pole
> I thank whatever gods may be
>   For my unconquerable soul.

So wrote W. E. Henley in 1875 after twenty painful months in hospital and the amputation of a tubercular leg. This is the stoic mood of agnostic heroism. The blackness of the night, the lack of any assurance of anything but extinction after death, makes the heroic stance more urgent:

> 'Empty vessel, garment cast,
> We that wore you long shall last.
> – Another night, another day.'
> So my bones within me say.
>
> Therefore they shall do my will
> Today while I am master still,

And flesh and soul, now both are strong,
Shall hale the sullen slaves along,

Before this fire of sense decay,
This smoke of thought blow clean away,
And leave with ancient night alone
The stedfast and enduring bone.

That, of course, is Housman, in *A Shropshire Lad* (1896). But if nothingness lies in wait for us, it does not mean for Housman, any more than it meant for Hardy, that destiny is neutral and there is a fifty-fifty chance of things going right. Though Housman might have said as Hardy said in 1866:

These purblind Doomsters had as readily strown
Blisses about my pilgrimage as pain

he shared with the older poet the view that in fact, in the younger poet's words, 'Luck's a chance, but trouble's sure.' He summed it up most effectively in the ninth poem of *Last Poems* (1922):

The troubles of our proud and angry dust
Are from eternity and shall not fail.
Bear them we can, and if we can we must.
Shoulder the sky, my lad, and drink your ale.

There are, however, two passages from Housman's prose

which illustrate most clearly of all both the late nineteenth-century stoical attitude and something of what lies behind it in earlier Victorian thought. The first comes from his introductory lecture as Professor of Latin at University College, London, delivered in October 1892:

> I will not say, as Prof. Tyndall has somewhere said, that all happiness belongs to him who can say from his heart 'I covet truth'. Entire happiness is not attainable either by this or by any other method. Nay it may be urged on the contrary that the pursuit of truth in some directions is even injurious to happiness, because it compels us to take leave of delusions which were pleasant while they lasted. It may be urged that the light shed on the origins and destiny of man by the pursuit of truth in some directions is not altogether a cheerful light. It may be urged that man stands today in the position of one who has been reared from his cradle as the child of a noble race and the heir to great possessions, and who finds at his coming of age that he has been deceived alike as to his origin and his expectations; that he neither springs of the high lineage he fancied, nor will inherit the vast estate he looked for, but must put off his towering pride, and contract his boundless hopes, and begin the world anew from a lower level: . . .

Darwinism was made by some into a foundation for a belief in progress; but here we find the Darwinian view of the descent of man combining with a disillusion with the earlier Victorian view of progress to serve as an example of the unhappiness that can be caused by truth. Man's origins and his expectations have both been misrepresented; the truth about both is not comforting. It is interesting that George Eliot, whose scepticism was never disillusion and who found a way of combining unbelief with moral fervour, was not one of those whose loss of faith was produced by Lyell or Darwin. 'It is characteristic of her,' wrote Humphrey House, 'that she lost her belief in dogmatic Christianity in rather a conservative style, in rather an old-fashioned context. The first phase of her infidelity was not brought on by Strauss or any other German rationalist, nor by fossils and monkeys and shellfish; it was rather brought on by the literary-historical tradition of the English eighteenth century.' This is perhaps one clue to the difference between the results of her unbelief and those of other Victorians. The old-fashioned sceptics may have lost their belief in dogmatic religion, but they never lost their faith in reason or in human nature. The new-fashioned scepticism was more radical, and it often led to the kind of scepticism that is classically illustrated in the second of my two Housman prose quotations, this time from the preface to his edition of Manilius (1903):

> To believe that wherever a best MS. gives possible readings it gives true readings, and that only where it gives impossible readings does it give false readings, is to believe that an incompetent editor is the darling of Providence, which has given its angels charge over him lest at any time his sloth and folly should produce their natural results and incur their appropriate penalty. Chance and the common course of nature will not bring it to pass that the readings of a MS. are right wherever they are possible and impossible wherever they are wrong: that needs divine intervention; and when one considers the history of man and the spectacle of the universe I hope one may say without impiety that divine intervention might have been better employed elsewhere. How the world is managed,

and why it was created, I cannot tell; but it is no feather-bed for the repose of sluggards.

Edmund Wilson was the first to point to this remarkable last sentence. But even he did not ask why Housman should have taken it to be the one certainty knowable by him that the world is no feather-bed for the repose of sluggards. Is this because of the survival of the fittest, the necessity for a continual struggle if survival is to be assured? But the whole point of this passage is that the stupid and intellectually indolent editors got away with it – until Housman arrived to expose them. Some sluggards have had a remarkably good time. But they *shouldn't* have had a good time; it was wrong for them to have idled their days away. Housman does not say why. The sceptic as self-indulgent dandy has had a long history. But the nonconformist conscience intervened decisively in English history at an early enough period to make it impossible for a sceptic such as Housman to use his scepticism as a passport to hedonism. Of course there were deep personal reasons for Housman's pessimism, as those acquainted with the details of his biography are aware. But that he chose an activist stoicism rather than passive gloom must have been due in some measure to the spirit of the age.

In the first chapter of his interesting book on W. E. Henley,[1] Jerome Buckley sketches a history of nineteenth-century activist stoicism as a background to Henley's view of his 'unconquerable soul'. He pinpoints the distinction

[1] Jerome Hamilton Buckley: *William Ernest Henley, A Study in the 'Counter-Decadence' of the 'Nineties.* Princeton, 1945.

between the moral and religious activists such as Carlyle and, on a lower level, Charles Kingsley, and the stoic activists for whom proud endurance of whatever fate sent was an end in itself, by quoting from a sermon of Kingsley's published the year before Henley wrote *Invictus*. Here is Kingsley:

> Some here, surely, have read Epictetus, the heathen whose thought most exactly coincides with that of the Psalmist. If so, do they not see what enabled him, the slave of Nero's minions, to *assert himself, and his own unconquerable personality*; *to defy circumstance*; and to preserve his own calm, his own honour, his own purity, amid a degradation which might well have driven a good man to suicide? And was it not this – The intensity of his faith in God?

Buckley points out that in phrasing this passage anticipates *Invictus*, though Henley's poem altogether lacks the trust in a divine Benevolence which justifies the kind of endurance praised by Kingsley. In *Invictus* 'the poet stands alone, a defiant agnostic, exultant in his strong free will, whatever gods may be'.

What distinguishes Byron's activism from that of later nineteenth-century writers is precisely that Byron was rooted in a pre-evangelical sensibility: the Byronic hero, for all his melodramatic gloom, for all his often nameless guilt, exhibited a *bravura*, a sort of moral dandyism, that was equally different from the earnest heroics of Henley and the stoical pessimism of Housman. One is tempted to say that early nineteenth-century evangelical Christianity marked a watershed in English sensibility. Even after Darwin and the higher criticism of the Bible had between them aroused all sorts of religious doubts, strenuousness remained an ideal for its own sake. Seventeenth-century Puritanism seems, oddly enough, to have left no such legacy to the eighteenth century. The eighteenth-century doctrine of the moral sense was the least strenuous of moral creeds, based as it was on the view that man had an innate taste for morality comparable to his aesthetic tastes. This remains true in spite of what Louis Bredvold has called, in a famous essay, 'the gloom of the Tory satirists' in the earlier part of the century. The Tory satirists did not believe in a meaningless darkness out of which men came and into which they were doomed to disappear, nor were they sceptical about the principles on which the world was governed. The darkness they attacked was, in Bredvold's words, 'a mundane darkness conjured up by human folly and knavery.' Men, not the government of the world, were to blame. Nor was the self-induced melancholy of the eighteenth-century 'graveyard poets' in any way comparable to the mood of the late nineteenth-century sceptical stoics. It is significant that one of the most savage essays ever written by George Eliot was an attack on Young's *Night Thoughts* for its superficiality and lack of truth to his own vision.

The fact is that in late nineteenth-century English literature we come up again and again against a phenomenon that is not easily paralleled in earlier English literature – this mood of what might be called sceptical stoicism combined with sceptical activism. Kipling – who is a prime exhibit here – summed it up in a poem written during the First World War:

The game is more than the player of the game,
And the ship is more than the crew!

But no; even this does not really sum it up. For what Kipling really seems to have meant was that the game was more than the *object* of the game and the ship more than the nature and purpose of the *journey*.

Kipling is a particularly interesting case because there are clear signs in much of his work of an evangelical sensibility turned to the contemplation of empire. Writing of Lord Milner and his 'kindergarten' he could praise them as doing God's work:

These at labour make no sign,
More than planets, tides or years
Which discover God's design,
Not our hopes and not our fears;
Nor in aught they gain or lose
Seek a triumph or excuse!

For, so the Ark be borne to Zion, who
Heeds how they perished or were paid that bore it?
For, so the Shrine abide, what shame – what pride –
If we, the priests, were bound or crowned before it?
(*The Pro-Consuls*)

Yet even here the suggestion is that the individuals who do God's work do it with no hope of reward of any sort. Now selflessness is, of course, an important element in any concept of religious duty, but it is only a relative selflessness. The gaining of one's own soul was the ultimate object, however much one wished to convert others or to live a life of Christian charity. The more one reads Kipling the more one realizes that often when he preaches strenuous endeavour there is no ultimate object. When in 1899 he urged the United States to take up the White Man's Burden in the Philippines he did not claim that it was the sake of improving the lot of the Filipinos – it was in order to test the white man's endurance and give him a strenuous work-out:

> Take up the White Man's burden –
> Have done with childish days –
> The lightly proffered laurel,
> The easy, ungrudged praise.
> Come now, to search your manhood
> Through all the thankless years,
> Cold-edged with dear-bought wisdom,
> The judgment of your peers!

They will be 'thankless' years. Imperialists get no thanks for what they do and indeed – Kipling does go as far as this – what they do may not in the long run be worth doing for itself at all. For it is bound to be undone in time. Kipling was fascinated by the last days of the Roman Empire in Britain, with the civilizing mission of the Romans failing and all to do again after the barbarians conquered:

> Her sentries pass on – that is all
> And we gather behind them in hordes,

And plot to reconquer the Wall,
  With only our tongues for our swords.
    (*A Pict Song*, in *Puck of Pook's Hill*)

We may today deplore Kipling's imperialist view that Indians and Africans would never be able to govern themselves; but he asserts it in order to demonstrate the futility of imperialism, which will not in the long run achieve anything. Yet Englishmen must go on testing themselves in this way, and the private soldier on the Indian frontier must go on leading a life of bitter discipline and restraint in the service of the distant Widow at Windsor who understands the realities of her imperialist policies no more than they understand what forces have sent them to lead this life of endurance in India.

'Ave you 'eard o' the Widow at Windsor
  With a hairy gold crown on 'er 'ead?
She 'as ships on the foam – she 'as millions at 'ome,
  An' she pays us poor beggars in red.
    (Ow, poor beggars in red!)
There's 'er nick on the cavalry 'orses,
  There's 'er mark on the medical stores –
An' 'er troopers you'll find with a fair wind be'ind
That takes us to various wars.
  (Poor beggars! – barbarious wars!)
  Then 'ere's to the Widow at Windsor,
  An' 'ere's to the stores an' the guns,
The men an' the 'orses what makes up the forces

O' Missis Victorier's sons.
(Poor beggars! Victorier's sons!)
(*The Widow at Windsor*)

It is instructive to set this pretty grimly realistic stanza about the truth of imperialism beside a paragraph from Kipling's story 'On the City Wall' in *Soldiers Three*:

> Year by year England sends out fresh drafts for the first fighting-line, which is officially called the Indian Civil Service. These die, or kill themselves by overwork, or are worried to death, or broken in health and hope in order that the land may be protected from death and sickness, famine and war, and may eventually become capable of standing alone. It will never stand alone, but the idea is a pretty one, and men are willing to die for it, and yearly the work of pushing and coaxing and scolding and petting the country into good living goes forward. If an advance be made all credit is given to the native, while the Englishmen stand back and wipe their foreheads. If a failure occurs the Englishmen step forward and take the blame. Overmuch tenderness of this kind has bred a strong belief among many natives that the native is capable of administering the country, and many devout Englishmen believe this also, because the theory is stated in beautiful English with the latest political colour.

In the end, the endurance of the Englishmen in India will go for nothing. 'It is a hard law,' Kipling wrote in *Letters of Travel* (1892–1913) 'but an old one – Rome died learning it, as our western civilization may die – that if you give any man anything that he had not painfully earned for himself, you may infallibly make him or his descendants your devoted enemies.' Imperialism is thus self-defeating, its real purpose evidently to test the endurance of the imperialists. The British Empire will go the way of the Roman Empire. I do not remember ever having seen it noticed how odd it is that in his famous *Recessional* of 1897 Kipling paints a vivid picture of the dissolution of the British Empire:

> Far-called, our navies melt away;
> On dune and headland sinks the fire:
> Lo, all our pomp of yesterday
> Is one with Nineveh and Tyre!

One is reminded of Housman's

> Then, 'twas before my time, the Roman
> At yonder heaving hill would stare:
> The blood that warms an English yeoman,
> The thoughts that hurt him, they were there. . . .
>
> The gale, it plies the sapling double,
> It blows so hard, 'twill soon be gone:
> To-day the Roman and his trouble
> Are ashes under Uricon.
>
> (*A Shropshire Lad: XXXI*)

Housman, too, shared Kipling's vision of the soldier of the Queen quietly doing his desperate duty:

The Queen she sent to look for me,
   The sergeant he did say,
'Young man, a soldier will you be
   For thirteen pence a day?'

For thirteen pence a day did I
   Take off the things I wore
And I have marched to where I lie,
   And I shall march no more. . . .

(*Last Poems: Grenadier*)

Kipling could put it more grimly:

If your officer's dead and the sergeants look white,
Remember it's ruin to run from a fight:
So take open order, lie down, and sit tight,
   And wait for supports like a soldier.
     Wait, wait, wait like a soldier . . .

When you're wounded and left on Afghanistan's plains,
And the women come out to cut up what remains,
Jest roll to your rifle and blow out your brains
   An' go to your Gawd like a soldier.
     Go, go, go like a soldier,
     Go, go, go like a soldier,
     Go, go, go like a soldier,
       So-oldier *of* the Queen!

So for Kipling imperial dominion will be self-defeating in the end, yet one must go on paying a terrible price for it:

We have fed our sea for a thousand years
And she calls us, still unfed,
Though there's never a wave of all her waves
But marks our English dead:
We have strewed our best to the weed's unrest,
To the shark and the sheering gull.
If blood be the price of admiralty,
Lord God, we ha' paid in full! . . .

We must feed our sea for a thousand years,
For that is our doom and pride,
As it was when they sailed with the *Golden Hind*,
Or the wreck that struck last tide –
Or the wreck that lies on the spouting reef
Where the ghastly blue-lights flare.
If blood be the price of admiralty,
If blood be the price of admiralty,
If blood be the price of admiralty,
Lord God, we ha' bought it fair!

(*A Song of the English*)

Alan Sandison, in an important essay on Kipling which appeared in *Kipling's Mind and Art* edited by Andrew Rutherford,[1] has described the subalterns of Kipling's Indian stories as 'drawn from actuality by a peculiarly Stoic mind', and he provides many examples of this stoicism from the stories. The British Administrator in India, as Kipling sees him, 'has at his core a terrible irony: he who would

[1] Edinburgh, 1964.

"administer" and rule this vast mass is himself the victim. Nor could it ever be otherwise. The British work in India was a huge macabre joke which Kipling and a few – but only a few – of his characters saw. In the light of this, one's primary duty was only superficially to the Queen-Empress: fundamentally, it was to one's own moral integrity.' And Sandison concludes by insisting that '*politique*, whether in the wider sense or in the narrower one of a shallow and ephemeral political idea, is neither the measure nor the source of his artistic vision. That was based on something much more vital, much more enduring – an acute awareness of man's essential isolation and an agonized consciousness of the razor edge on which he must balance to sustain his moment of existence.'

No two writers could be more different than George Eliot and Rudyard Kipling, but Kipling's deepest insights as an artist were summed up by those famous words about God, Immortality and Duty which George Eliot spoke to F. W. H. Myers in the Fellows' Garden of Trinity on a rainy May evening in 1873. Yet George Eliot's view of the imperative nature of duty was bound up with her rational, humanist attitude towards human behaviour and human goals. Kipling's, in the last analysis, was not. What he called England's 'pride and doom' was a fatal obligation laid on her for no ultimate rational purpose. In spite of some similarities, I do not think that this underlying attitude of Kipling's is traceable back to the tradition of stoic fatalism that John Livingstone Lowes saw as stemming from *Beowulf* and *The Battle of Maldon*. The warrior code that was acted out in the last desperate stand at Maldon was a code which related human behaviour to human ideals and to a view of man's place in the scheme of things. And Anglo-Saxon fatalism is bound up with a sense of human destiny being worked out by something or someone beyond man: there is, therefore, an ultimate meaning to it, even if men cannot see that meaning. It is the ultimate emptiness of Kipling's world that is so terrifying: for all his insistence on codes, on the Law, on patterns of discipline, on the importance of the in-group and the secret society, for all his awareness of the ultimate sanctions that keep society from going over the edge – an awareness that has been pointed out by Noël Annan, who sees Kipling as a pioneer sociologist among English creative writers – there is something very like nihilism at the heart of his work.

Kipling has been compared in this respect to Conrad. But Conrad is really much more ambivalent in his attitude to society than Kipling, for whom morality, as Annan pointed out, was an entirely social product and at least served the end of survival of a sort. At the end of 1898, when he was writing *Heart of Darkness*, Conrad wrote to R. B. Cunninghame Graham: 'L'homme est un animal méchant. Sa méchanceté doit être organisée. Le crime est une condition nécessaire de l'existence organisée. La société est essentiellement criminelle – ou elle n'existerait pas. C'est l'égoïsme qui sauve tout – absolument tout – tout ce que nous abhorrons, tout ce que nous aimons.' ('Man is a wicked animal. His wickedness must be organized. Crime is a necessary condition of organized existence. Society is essentially criminal – or it wouldn't exist. It is egoism that saves everything – absolutely everything – everything that we hate, everything that we love.') Conrad professed to find in the simple seaman's code of fidelity, loyalty, endurance, a sufficient basis for his ethics, but though he sometimes wrote in these terms in articles and prefaces the insights provided by his finest work belie this view. *Nostromo* is an admirable commentary on and qualification of the observations he made to Cunninghame Graham. In that novel we are presented with a hopeless paradox: society is necessary but it corrupts, loneliness is desirable but it destroys. The 'material interests' which in the end enslave Charles Gould and destroy his relationship with his wife are the precise opposite of the impulse to withdrawal and isolation which, when accidentally achieved, drive Decoud to suicide. And between these two extremes the novel shows a most subtle and complex range of stances, from crude selfishness to impractical idealism. But however we look at the novel, the pessimism remains deep and inescapable. Social man is corrupt and destructive of others; individual man is self-destructive. If we subsume others' needs to our own imaginative needs and impulses we jump as Lord Jim jumped. If we are trapped into trying to mediate between an isolated sense of identity and an outgoing sense of community, like Razumov in *Under Western Eyes*, we destroy ourselves and others. If we use our relations with others purely to serve our own aloof purposes, like most of the characters in *The Secret Agent*, the end result is even more destructive. Moral idealism can in certain conditions backfire and produce the reverse of itself, as with Mr Kurtz in *Heart of Darkness*. And at any time the individual is in danger of recognizing himself in someone who appears at first sight to be his moral opposite – this theme is very common in Conrad. Only the unimaginative, lonely, unswerving, enduring Captain McWhirr, alone in a typhoon in the China Sea and steering his craft through appalling dangers by doggedly sticking to the rule book, wins through without obvious disillusion or self-destruction. He is lucky in never having met circumstances to which his simple seaman's code was inapplicable, and in his lack of imagination which would make it impossible for him to realize if in fact it was inapplicable. His is the kind of egoism that saves.

Conrad, as a Pole turned Englishman, had his special problems, and the underlying pessimism of his work is clearly related to these. Yet in the end something very like the activist stoicism which I have described earlier emerges from his novels as the only way of confronting life. Such an attitude will not solve problems, for in Conrad's most deeply felt novels the real problems are insoluble. But it will enable man to come to terms with himself. This is less faith in an ideal (though Conrad sometimes wrote as though it was) so much as a posture, a stance. 'Carry on regardless.' This now comic phrase would have been accepted, or at least its implications would have been accepted, equally by Conrad, Kipling and Housman.

All this is related to the traditional British 'stiff upper lip' attitude, but it is worth pausing for a moment to observe that this attitude is not as traditionally British as is sometimes supposed and in fact emerges fully only in the latter part of the nineteenth century. This surely must have something to do with the ethos of the English Public School, which really came into flower at this period. Further, the peculiar functionlessness of late nineteenth-century stoic activism may well be related to the schoolboy's shyness of confessing to ideals and ultimate moral objectives – a shyness reflected many times in Kipling's stories. Is there some relation here also to the much discussed tradition of British pragmatism, to British suspicion of neat formulations of philosophical ends (something to be left to the abstractly logical minds of Frenchmen and other foreigners)? Pragmatism, in the popular sense, means getting things done without bothering too much about the theory behind it all. This is not very far away from the view that one should endure, carry on, stick it out, for no definable ultimate objective. Endurance is a substitute for understanding:

> And how am I to face the odds
> Of man's bedevilment and God's?
> I, a stranger and afraid
> In a world I never made.
> They will be master, right or wrong;
> Though both are foolish, both are strong.
> And since, my soul, we cannot fly
> To Saturn nor to Mercury,
> Keep we must, if keep we can,
> These foreign laws of God or man.
>
> (Housman, *Last Poems: XII*)

All this has taken us very far away from George Eliot, whose ability to reconcile a belief in the absoluteness of duty with scepticism about God and immortality was one of my starting points. For her, endurance was no substitute for understanding, but moral behaviour was the means to clearly viewed human ends. It is the strong rational element of George Eliot's view that steadily declines as the century progresses, at least among the writers I have been discussing. One might think that the humane and sensitive rational utilitarianism of John Stuart Mill would have provided a firm ethical base for late nineteenth-century writers, but it is difficult to think of any significant writer of the end of the century who can be said to have based himself on Mill's philosophy. The nonconformist conscience survived both faith and reason: what the Victorians produced in unprecedented quantities was *worry*.

Let us now go back to another ancestor of late Victorian stoicism. Matthew Arnold referred with admiration to Epictetus twenty-six years before Kingsley claimed him as of one mind with the Psalmist.

Who prop, thou ask'st, in these bad days, my mind?

Arnold asked his friend Clough in a sonnet written in 1848. The first of the props was Homer. But also

> Much he, whose friendship I not long since won,
> That halting slave, who in Nicopolis
> Taught Arrian, when Vespasian's brutal son
> Cleared Rome of what most shamed him.

He is referring, in an obliquely Miltonic style, to Epictetus the Stoic philosopher. The third in the trilogy was Sophocles

> Who saw life steadily and saw it whole.

Some three years later he was thinking of Sophocles again, as he watched the waves breaking on Dover Beach:

> Listen! you hear the grating roar
> Of pebbles which the waves draw back, and fling,
> At their return, up the high strand,
> Begin, and cease, and then again begin,
> With tremulous cadence slow, and bring
> The eternal note of sadness in.
>
> Sophocles long ago
> Heard it on the Aegean, and it brought
> Into his mind the turbid ebb and flow
> Of human misery; we
> Find also in the sound a thought,
> Hearing it by this distant northern sea.
>
> The Sea of Faith
> Was once, too, at the full, and round earth's shore
> Lay like the folds of a bright girdle furled.
> But now I only hear
> Its melancholy, long, withdrawing roar,
> Retreating, to the breath
> Of the night-wind, down the vast edges drear
> And naked shingles of the world.

Ah, love, let us be true
To one another! for the world, which seems
To lie before us like a land of dreams,
So various, so beautiful, so new,
Hath really neither joy, nor love, nor light,
Nor certitude, nor peace, nor help for pain;
And we are here as on a darkling plain
Swept with confused alarms of struggle and flight,
Where ignorant armies clash by night.

This is a classic statement of a certain kind of Victorian loss of faith, all the more so since the fact of loss of faith is explicitly stated and the sense of melancholy meaninglessness in the world directly attributed to it. But instead of the call to endure, there is the call to depend on a personal relationship. In a brief but seminal essay on Victorian doubt first broadcast by the BBC in 1948 and reprinted in his posthumous collection of essays, *All in Due Time,*[1] Humphrey House saw *Dover Beach* as a symptom of something very important in Victorian thought and feeling:

> The more I read of the early- and mid-Victorians, the more I see anxiety and worry as a leading clue to understanding them. They were not complacent compromisers. They were trying to hold together incompatible opposites, and they worried because they failed. They clung to an immortality that should not include the possible justice of Eternal Punishment; they wanted a system of administra-

[1] London, 1955.

> tion which should be efficient without expense; in face of repeated and ferocious strikes and riots, they clung to the doctrine that the interests of employers and employed were identical. They knew such things as these were incompatibles; they worried because they could neither reconcile them nor move on to other terms of thought. They worried about immortality, they worried about sex, they worried about politics and money. They were indeed caught between two worlds. It fell to them to begin the adjustment of the whole complex human organisation, personal and political. It fell to them to adjust it to an environment that was utterly new in the history of the race. It is not surprising if, to support life at all, they turned to (among other things) an intensification of personal relationships and an unbalanced exaggeration of domestic virtues.

It can be argued that this 'intensification of personal relationships' is an aspect of the Romantic movement and begins well before the Victorian age of anxiety. But, though this is true, House put his finger on something important here. Romantic exploration of personal relationships was a means of discovering truth; the kind that House was talking about was a way of escape from a world in which truth was undiscoverable and one fell back on *égoïsme à deux*. 'Ah, love, let us be true to one another' – *because* there are no other certain truths. Personal relationships are thus given an enormous, indeed an intolerable role to play. They must provide all human values. And is this not one of the great themes of the late nineteenth and early twentieth-century novel from James to Lawrence? The reason why in the end John Marcher, in *The Beast in the Jungle*, found that he had lived a totally meaningless life was because he had refused the one way to discover value in living – this was 'intensification of personal relationships'. He could have escaped from nothingness: 'The escape would have been to love her.'

To create your personal breakwater against a tide of nothingness is not stoicism, but one can see the relation between this and the creation of a world of values (or quasi-values) by stoic activism, by endurance, by sticking it out. Yet there is another side to the mood and significance of *Dover Beach*. House talked about 'an intensification of personal relationships and an unbalanced exaggeration of domestic virtues' as a Victorian way of escape. But if domestic relations stand at the further side of *égoïsme à deux*, total withdrawal into oneself, pure isolated introspection, stands at the inner side. This too had been a romantic refuge from insoluble problems:

> then on the shore
> Of the wide world I stand alone, and think
> Till love and fame to nothingness do sink.

Keats, however, did have the specific problem of the prospect of his own early death to worry about in this sonnet. The worries of Arnold and Tennyson were more generalized. Arnold on Dover Beach extends Keats's sad-sweet mood of introspection only slightly outwards, to include one other person. Tennyson loved to retreat into a similar mood of melancholy isolation, in which the work and play of the outside world represented a quite alien environment:

> O, well for the fisherman's boy,
> That he shouts with his sister at play!
> O, well for the sailor lad,
> That he sings in his boat on the bay!
>
> And the stately ships go on
> To their haven under the hill; . . .

Or, to take one more example, there are the well-known lines from *In Memoriam*:

> He is not here; but far away
> The noise of life begins again,
> And ghastly through the drizzling rain
> On the bald street breaks the blank day.

The workday world has nothing to do with the poet, who hugs his isolation. And even the mood of mourning for a dead person is used as a means of retreating inwards to oneself, using a personal grief in order to subsume all the insoluble problems of the world in a blanket of elegiac self-indulgence. (Once you have done that, and established the feeling self as the only relevant criterion, you can emerge later and announce as satisfactorily proved any belief you like, simply in terms of personal mood or conviction. That is how Tennyson solved his intellectual problem in *In Memoriam*.)

So if problems of faith could produce stoic activism, they could also produce meditative passivity. In Arnold there are traces of both. He believed in action but was temperamentally led to meditation: the end of *Sohrab and Rustum*, conceived as an episode in an epic, is pure mood poetry, achieved by turning from the human actors to the river and the sky. (So Tennyson kept slipping from the mode of action to the mode of elegy in his Arthurian poems.) Yet Arnold's poetry shows also the reverse process. *Rugby Chapel* opens with what might be called standard mid-Victorian elegiac imagery:

> Coldly, sadly descends
> The autumn-evening. The field
> Strewn with its dank yellow drifts
> Of withered leaves, and the elms
> Fade into dimness apace,
> Silent; hardly a shout
> From a few boys late at their play!

(Those late-playing boys have no more connexion with the speaker than Tennyson's fisherman's boy at play with his sister.) But in the end the evangelical note, the note of endurance and endeavour and struggle, sounds out:

> Eyes rekindling, and prayers,
> Follow your steps as ye go.
> Ye fill up the gaps in our files,
> Strengthen the wavering line,

Stablish, continue our march,
On, to the bound of the waste,
On, to the City of God.

In Arnold's moral and intellectual world the phrase 'City of God' had no very precise connotation. It is employed here as little more than an obeisance to the public school code of carrying on. I have no wish to belittle Arnold, who was a fine poet, but in terms of the history of attitudes these lines seem connected not only with Kipling's

The game is more than the player of the game,
And the ship is more than the crew!

but also with Sir Henry Newbolt's

The sand of the desert is sodden red, –
Red with the wreck of a square that broke; –
The gatling's jammed and the colonel dead,
And the regiment blind with the dust and smoke.
The river of death has brimmed its banks
And England's far and honour a name,
But the voice of a schoolboy rallies the ranks:
'Play up! play up! and play the game!'

(*Vitai Lampada*)

I am trying to suggest that there *is* a line between Arnold and the tradition of stoic activism, a vision which finds its superbly vulgar expression in Newbolt's rhetorical verse.

And Tennyson, too, had his moods of undefined activism:

> that which we are, we are;
> One equal temper of heroic hearts,
> Made weak by time and fate, but strong in will
> To strive, to seek, to find, and not to yield.
> (*Ulysses*)

Not that it is critically profitable to associate poems of such different quality and basic temper. Yet there is something here for the historian of attitudes. The English Public School is involved in all three extracts I have quoted. Thomas Arnold was responsible for much more than he or his son ever knew.

The real reason, however, why I went back to Arnold and Tennyson after discussing Housman, Kipling and Conrad was to illustrate the source of a late nineteenth-century attitude that runs parallel to that of stoic activism. Even if there are traces of the latter view in Arnold and Tennyson, and even if Arnold deplored poems 'in which suffering finds no vent in action', the most characteristic mood of both these poets is one of what we might call relished melancholy. And mood poetry of this kind lies behind an important aspect of the late nineteenth-century aesthetic movement. This mood responded to the same doubts and uncertainties that oppressed Hardy and Housman and others but the response took the form of total refuge in inward feelings. One normally contrasts the aesthetes with activists like Henley and Kipling – and indeed their own contemporaries pointed the contrast – but there is a curious parallel between art for art's sake and endurance for endurance' sake. The ultimately objectless nature of the Kiplingesque code of law and duty has, one might even say, an aesthetic beauty, a beauty deriving from its inner consistency and not from what Joyce would have called any 'kinetic' element, any element of effectively purposeful action towards a rational end. But whether one concedes the similarities or not, one cannot help seeing that the creed (in so far as it was a coherent creed) of the late nineteenth-century aesthetes was a response to the same doubts of ultimate values and objectives that we find in Housman and the other writers I discussed with him. The situation is sometimes expressed more melodramatically, as in Ernest Dowson's poem *A Last Word*:

> Let us go hence: the night is now at hand;
> The day is overworn, the birds all flown;
> And we have reaped the crops the gods have sown;
> Despair and death; deep darkness o'er the land,
> Broods like an owl; . . .

In this kind of poetry the expression of despair is itself a compensation for despair, a sort of emotional luxuriousness which is the last refuge of the poet who lacks altogether a world of external values. Pater, of course, was the prophet here, recommending in that famous Conclusion to *The Renaissance* the intensification of experience for its own sake, and preaching art as the way to such intensification. 'For art comes to you proposing frankly to give nothing but the highest quality to your moments as they pass, and simply for those moments' sake.' The ambiguous word here is 'highest', which sounds vaguely ethical but isn't – indeed it has no specific normative content, only an area of suggestion.

When Oscar Wilde, in the Preface to *The Picture of Dorian Gray*, asserted that 'all art is quite useless' he was not merely indulging in his fondness for startling paradoxes. In terms of the aesthetic creed there is no way in which to define usefulness. So of course all art is quite useless. Usefulness as a term depends on some system of objective values, some view of means and ends. The aesthetic view of value is entirely solipsistic: all the aesthete seeks is to multiply and diversify inward personal experience. Even in talking politics, Wilde never escaped from this. 'The chief advantage that would result from the establishment of Socialism,' wrote Wilde in the opening paragraph of *The Soul of Man Under Socialism*, 'is, undoubtedly, the fact that Socialism would relieve us from that sordid necessity of living for others which, in the present condition of things, presses so hardly upon almost everybody.' To Wilde, Socialism was valuable because it would release the individual to dwell with full enjoyment in the world of Paterian variety and intensity of inner experience. The curious paradox about Wilde is that even when preaching the Paterian creed at its most extreme and hailing the useless and solipsistic nature of art, he is led by some lurking puritanism in his nature to sneak in a traditional moral. Charles Whibley no doubt overstated the case when he said that *The Picture of Dorian Gray* contained 'lots of morality and no art', but one sees what he meant. The Paterian search for experience is shown in this story to be corrupting on traditional moral standards and undesirable for that reason. It is surprising that Wilde did not seem to know what a conventionally moral work he had produced, positively philistine, indeed, in its identification of new aesthetic experience with moral evil.

Still, Wilde was not usually on that side; more characteristic of him was his desire to reduce all life to artifice, to which no general concepts of value could apply. 'No artist has ethical sympathies. An ethical sympathy in an artist is an unpardonable mannerism of style.' This is more than a piece of witty provocation: it is the clue to what Wilde actually does, for example, in *The Importance of Being Earnest*. The wit of this play lies precisely in its reduction of life to artifice, its wilful ignoring of all human values to concentrate on the *style* with which situations are acted out. 'To be born, or at any rate bred, in a hand-bag, whether it had handles or not, seems to me to display a contempt for the ordinary decencies of family life that reminds one of the worst excesses of the French Revolution.' Lady Bracknell's well-known lines are funny in a very special way: they reduce the significance of all human actions to style, to a code played according to rules. And rules are by definition arbitrary. The point about a game is that it is played according to the rules of that game, not according to eternal values or verities; and once you start doubting the rules the game cannot go on. (Huizinga discusses this very well in his *Homo Ludens: A Study of the Play Element in Culture*.)

Another element in play is often its competitiveness. In Wilde's plays we see both elements. Social life is conducted according to the rules of the game, and wit results from people applying these rules with competitive ingenuity. We are thus back to Kipling's

> The game is more than the player of the game,
> And the ship is more than the crew!

When Cecily says: 'I pity any poor woman whose husband is not called Ernest,' she is talking meaningless nonsense in any human terms that go outside the play, but according to the competitive rules observed by all the characters in the play she is doing very well. This is not to deny the humour of these plays; it is simply to indicate the nature and source of that humour.

The reduction of interesting human situations to competitive essays in style played according to internally consistent but wholly arbitrary rules produces, then, the Wildean comedy. Wildean wit is not really the same as the wit of Restoration comedy, for although Restoration comedy also has its competitive wit-combats these rarely have the effect of reducing all life to style. In Wycherley there is a moral-satiric element. In Congreve, where the wit-combats seem sometimes most like those of Wilde, the author is nevertheless genuinely concerned to present a pattern of relationships which indicate his view of the proper relationship between the sex and of the problems that arise in the conflict between the male and female attitudes to sex and between private desire and public reputation. Restoration comedy, one might almost say, represented a reaction from a surfeit of over-intent ethical argument, whereas Wildean comedy was a reaction to (but not against) generations of doubt and a gradual and worried accumulation of scepticism. If you only have to enjoy the competitive acting out of the necessarily arbitrary rules of the game, you don't have to worry about values. Children who, in the middle of a game, start questioning the rules and asking what the use of it all is, soon stop that particular game altogether.

We are used to contrasting the aesthetes and the activists, Wilde and Kipling, and thinking of them as representing opposite poles of late nineteenth-century thought. But they are closer to each other than might at first appear. Quite apart from the fact that Kipling's attitude at school was that of the aesthete who despised athletics, quite apart also from his relationship with Burne-Jones and family association with the Pre-Raphaelite movement, there is the fact that Kipling's view of his craft – indeed, of *any* craft – was an aesthetic one in the sense that it was removed from any consideration of an objective outside itself. McAndrew (in *McAndrew's Hymn*) celebrates his engines not because they enable the ship to get more quickly from one port to another but because they are things of ordered beauty:

The crank-throws give the double-bass, the feed pump
 sobs an' heaves,
An' now the main eccentrics start their quarrel on the
 sheaves:

Her time, her own appointed time, the rocking link-head
  bides,
Till – hear that note? – the rod's return whines glimmerin'
  through the guides.
They're all awa! True beat, full power, the clangin'
  chorus goes
Clear to the tunnel where they sit, my purrin' dynamoes.
Interdependence absolute, foreseen, ordained, decreed,
To work, Ye'll note, at any tilt an' every rate o' speed.
Fra' skylight-lift to furnace-bars, backed, bolted, braced
  an' stayed,
An' singin' like the mornin' Stars for joy that they are
  made; . . .

It is worth remembering, too, that W. E. Henley in his art criticism attacked purely representational and 'literary' painting and insisted on the significance of form – like his friend R. L. Stevenson whose advice to art students was: 'In your own art, bow your head over technique. Think of technique when you rise and when you go to bed. Forget purposes in the meanwhile; get to love technical processes; . . .'

'Forget purposes . . . get to love technical processes.' Kipling and Henley agreed with the aesthetes here. When, after Oscar Wilde's conviction, the British public hastened to assert its virility and heterosexuality by dropping the works of Wilde and his friends and seeking out those of Kipling and Henley, they were not going so far as they thought. Aestheticism and stoic activism can be seen as opposite sides of the same medal. It is an over-simplification to say that both represent attempts to compensate for a lost world of absolute value. Yet it is an over-simplification worth asserting, for the germ of truth which it contains is worth further exploration.

2

In my last lecture I observed that problems of faith could produce in nineteenth-century poets both stoic activism and passive melancholy, and I suggested that both of these could be found in Arnold. I pointed also to the mood of introspective trance-like meditation in a sonnet of Keats. And these poetic modes I distinguished in turn from the 'graveyard' school of the eighteenth century. There is another ancestor, or at least prototype, of late Victorian poetic attitudes whom I should like to call to witness at this point – not an English poet this time but the Italian Giacomo Leopardi. I have often thought that the concluding lines of the most famous of all his poems, *L'infinito*, distil that particular kind of broodiness that I have associated with the Victorian elegiac mode:

> Così tra questa
> Immensità s'annega il pensier mio:
> E il naufragar m'è dolce in questo mare.

'Thus in this immensity my thought is drowned: and shipwreck is sweet to me in this sea.' Leopardi was quite conscious of the role played by melancholy brooding in his poetry, and he distinguished it from the more robust attitude of the ancients. 'Non è propria de' tempi nostri altra poesia che la malinconica,' he wrote, 'nè altro tuono di poesia che questo, sopra qualunque subbietto ella possa essere.' 'No poetry other than melancholy poetry is proper to our age, no other poetic mood than this, whatever the subject.' Though there were cogent personal reasons for Leopardi's pessimism he too, as Tennyson and Arnold and Housman were to do, attributed it to a loss of faith in divinely guaranteed values:

> Non ha natura al seme
> dell'uom più stima o cura
> ch'alla formica: e se più rara in quello
> che nell'altra è la strage,
> non avvien ciò d'altronde
> fuor che l'uom sue prosapie ha men feconde.
>
> (*La ginestra*)

'Nature has no more respect or care for the seed of man than for the ant: and if destruction is less common with one than with the other, this comes from nothing else than man's lesser fertility in producing offspring.'
Or again, in *A sè stesso*:

> Amaro e noia
> la vita, altro mai nulla; . . .

'Life is bitterness and tedium, never anything else.'

It was while thinking about James Thomson's powerful picture of Melencolia [*sic*] at the end of his *City of*

Dreadful Night that I was reminded of Leopardi's *noia* – a more desperate state of mind, I cannot help feeling, than the related *ennui* of Baudelaire. Thomson discovered Leopardi in the 1860's, and though William Schaefer in his book on Thomson[1] does not attribute the English poet's rapid change from optimism to atheistic pessimism entirely to Leopardi's influence, some influence there clearly was. Thomson translated Leopardi's *Operette Morali* and *Pensieri* in the late 1860's and dedicated *The City of Dreadful Night and Other Poems* to him on its publication in 1880. Certainly the sense of complete nullity in the universe that Leopardi expressed so concisely in *A sè stesso* is identical with the feeling expressed in a different idiom by Thomson:

> I find no hint throughout the Universe
> Of good or ill, of blessing or of curse.

'Al gener nostro il fato non dona che il morire,' wrote Leopardi. 'To our species fate has granted only the gift of death.' The preacher in Thomson's City proclaims the identical news:

> And now at last authentic word I bring,
> Witnessed by every dead and living thing;
> Good tidings of great joy for you, for all:
> There is no God; no Fiend with names divine
> Made us and tortures us; if we must pine,
> It is to satiate no Being's gall . . .

[1] William Shaefer: *James Thomson (B.V.) : Beyond 'The City'*. Berkeley and Los Angeles, 1965.

This little life is all we must endure,
The grave's most holy peace is ever sure,
  We fall asleep and never wake again;
Nothing is of us but the mouldering flesh,
Whose elements dissolve and merge afresh
  In air, earth, water, plants, and other men . . .

O Brothers of sad lives! they are so brief;
A few short years must bring us all relief:
  Can we not bear these years of labouring breath?
But if you would not this poor life fulfil,
Lo, you are free to end it when you will,
  Without the fear of waking after death.

Yet, if the thought in Thomson's best-known poem is very like Leopardi's, the tone is quite different. It is different, too, from the tone of stoical endurance that we have seen in other late nineteenth-century poets. True, Melencolia, who presides over the City, is gazed upon by its inhabitants,

The strong to drink new strength of iron endurance,
The weak new terrors; all, renewed assurance
  And confirmation of the old despair.

The endurance drunk by the strong is neither Housman's nor Kipling's: it is of an altogether more rhetorical nature. And there is no ethical feeling in Thomson's poem, whereas the paradox of the coexistence of an ultimate scepticism with a deep sense of duty is to be found in these other writers.

Thomson is not a great poet and often not even a very good one. Even the poems of his earlier pantheistic vitalism, such as those included in *Sunday up the River*, his only other reasonably well-known work ('Gay shall be life's trip, my dear'; 'Thank God for Life!' 'Give a man a horse he can ride'), are curiously thin and tinny. *The City of Dreadful Night* stands out for its nightmare rhetoric, its larger-than-life-size masochistic gloom. It is not Hardyesque, because for one thing Hardy never lost a profound sense of the irony of circumstance, a sense which is never manifested in Thomson's poem. It has none of Housman's stoicism or Kipling's sense of law and duty. Thomson, in fact, is very much an odd man out in the picture I have been trying to draw. Under the influence of his friend Bradlaugh and of the rationalist journal *The National Reformer*, for which he wrote quite a lot, he became a professional atheist. His atheism does not seem to have been the *cause* of his pessimism: his was not the case of Tennyson and Arnold who *wanted* to believe, who suffered while they could not, and worked their way through to some kind of belief, however tenuous Arnold's theism may have really been. Far from finding belief in God and immortality necessary if life was to be faced, Thomson found, or professed to find, relief in being able to throw them overboard and so not to have to worry about reconciling the facts of experience with the planning of an omnipotent God. Nor, as Professor Schaefer has shown, can we attribute Thomson's pessimism to the death of an early love, a naïve assumption of virtually all previous biographers. It clearly had something to do with his alcoholism, but again there arises the question of which was cause and which effect. The interesting fact is that if, after reading the literature of late Victorian doubt and scepticism, after studying the effects on poets and novelists of Lyell and Darwin and the Higher Criticism of the Bible, we turn to *The City of Dreadful Night*, we are quite taken aback. Thomson does not have a Victorian kind of worry.

Nevertheless, Melencolia herself is a late Victorian figure. Though the human characters in *The City of Dreadful Night* do not adopt any of the Victorian attitudes I discussed in my last lecture, this 'stupendous' image, 'the bronze colossus of a winged Woman', is Necessity as well as Melancholy, and she (though not those over whom she presides) works on with that meaningless tenacity, that stubborn though sceptical endurance, which we have seen in Housman and Kipling:

> Baffled and beaten back she works on still,
>   Weary and sick of soul she works the more,
> Sustained by her indomitable will:
>   The hands shall fashion and the brain shall pore
> And all her sorrow shall be turned to labour,
> Till death the friend-foe piercing with his sabre
>   That mighty heart of hearts ends bitter war.

It would insult the dignity of this massive figure to recite to her at this point Newbolt's 'Play up, play up, and play the game!' Yet what is going on here is not so very unlike the final scene in Newbolt's poem or those many scenes in Kipling where soldiers stick it out to the end on distant frontiers for causes they do not understand. 'All the divinities have fled, and on high there dwells but an old woman with hands of iron and disconsolate heart – Necessity,' Thomson wrote in a revealing essay on Heine. Necessity's other name is Melencolia, and at the end of *The City of Dreadful Night* we encounter the extraordinary spectacle of Necessity herself sticking it out to the end through necessity. Baffled and beaten back, weary and sick of soul, she is yet 'sustained by her indomitable will' to carry on. In the face of the goddess Necessity herself behaving with stoical endurance, poor man can only despair. For in this poem, in a most curious reversal of late Victorian roles, stoic activism is not for man but for Fate.

Thomson had no very clear or consistent political views: his pessimistic atheism did not lead him to any specific reformist position with reference to social or political issues. Though he was anti-imperialist, anti-jingoist and vaguely republican in sympathies he was not a political activist. Pessimism is a conservative position, as can be seen very clearly in Conrad. Stoicism is a conservative stance, as can be seen equally clearly in Kipling. At the same time, scepticism about the basis of Victorian religion and morality could lead to a questioning of Victorian social institutions and modes of conduct. Interestingly enough, Thomson had made some frontal attacks on cherished Victorian ideals before he became a convinced atheist. He attacked Victorian respectability under the name of 'Bumbleism'. He attacked the Carlylean gospel of work in 1867, the year when he was becoming deeply involved with Leopardi. He called the

English passion for work 'an irrational idolatry' and explained Carlyle's cry of 'Work!' as 'simply the Imperative mood of a doctrine which, couched in the quiet Indicative, reads, "Mankind is a damned rascal".' The only object of such an imperative was to keep man overwhelmed and exhausted until he sank into the grave, 'impotent for further mischief'. The hero of Longfellow's *Excelsior* was an ineffable ass and an infernal idiot. 'What possible good could he do himself or anybody else by planting that banner with the very strange device on the top of that mountain?'

Thomson's attack on strenuousness as an ideal was aimed at something very deep in the English character. Some of its earlier origins have been traced in Tawney's *Religion and the Rise of Capitalism* but, as I suggested in my last lecture, it was given a new lease of life by late eighteenth- and early nineteenth-century evangelical Christianity which left a legacy of earnestness and endurance even to late Victorian sceptics. Though Matthew Arnold had attacked one kind of moral earnestness in *Culture and Anarchy*, his was not a frontal attack on earnestness and strenuousness as such, but rather an attempt to balance a necessary Hebraism by a compensating Hellenism. But Thomson here denied completely the value of what Arnold called Hebraism and in this he was at one with the position to be developed by the aesthetes and also by an important late Victorian writer who had no love for the aesthetes – Samuel Butler. Butler had in fact much more in common with Oscar Wilde than either realized. The former's remark in his *Notebooks* that 'the one serious conviction that a man should have is that nothing is to be taken too seriously' might have been made by Wilde. Both continually sniped at Victorian conventions and preconceptions. Wilde's sniping was not, however, serious warfare, because he needed those conventions for the proper play of his wit. No writer ever needed an artificial society more than Wilde. The wit of his plays depended on it. In his more serious writings (at least, of those before his trial and sentence) he tended to assume that a life of upper-class well-endowed hedonism was the most worth living. This is not very far from the life of moneyed dilettantism that the hero of *The Way of All Flesh* finally achieves, a life held up by Butler as the ideal.

Compared with Wilde's, however, Butler's ideal is incorrigibly middle class. Ernest Pontifex's (and his creator's) admiration for the effortless mindlessness of the upper-class Towneley is in sharp contrast to Wilde's association of aristocracy with wit, and arose from bourgeois envy of aristocratic grace. Yet Butler could challenge Victorian middle-class assumptions even more sharply than Wilde, for he could turn those assumptions against themselves and expose the double standard underlying the moral world of the Victorian business man:

> For most men, and most circumstances pleasure – tangible material prosperity in this world – is the safest test of virtue. Progress has ever been through the pleasures rather than through the extreme sharp virtues, and the most virtuous have leaned to excess rather than to asceticism. To use a commercial metaphor, competition is so keen, and the margin of profits has been cut down so closely

> that virtue cannot afford to throw any *bona fide* chance away, and must base her action rather on the actual moneying out of conduct than on a flattering prospectus. She will not therefore neglect – as some do who are prudent and economical enough in other matters – the important factor of our chance of escaping detection, or at any rate of our dying first. . . .
>
> Pleasure, after all, is a safer guide than either right or duty.

This is to put the hedonist position more strongly than ever Wilde put it. It is, in a way, a mocking version of Benthamism. But we note the centrality in it of the financial metaphor. Butler's concern with money, its inheritance, investment, accumulation, is almost obsessive. Though he attacked some of the most powerful of Victorian institutions – education, the church, the family – he had a positively Forsytean belief in the value of money, to an abundance of which he thought everybody had an absolute right. No parents and lots of money was his recipe for the good life: Towneley's parents, it will be remembered, had died in a drowning accident soon after his birth. 'Why should the generations overlap one another at all?' Butler asked in *The Way of All Flesh* (for Overton's voice is Butler's voice here as in many other places in the novel). 'Why cannot we be buried as eggs in neat little cells with ten or twenty thousand pounds each wrapped round us in Bank of England notes, and wake up, as the sphex wasp does, to find that its papa and mamma have not only left ample provision at its elbow, but have been eaten by sparrows some weeks before it began to live consciously on its own account?' Butler always believed that the primary function of a father was to bequeath money to his children. And money for him had a *moral* value. *The Way of All Flesh* is a *Bildungsroman:* it treats of the moral education of Ernest Pontifex. But that education is made possible only by the trust that his Aunt Alethea set up for him. He emerged after all his trials to find Alethea's legacy, now accumulated to £70,000, waiting to enable him to profit from his misfortunes and lead the good life.

It is interesting that Butler splits himself into two, as it were, in this novel: he is the narrator Mr Overton, Ernest's godfather and adviser, who speaks Butler's mature wisdom, and he is Ernest himself, who is educated by luck and hard experience to be the kind of rich, unmarried writer (a *homo unius libri*, as Butler himself was held to be, to his annoyance), moderately sceptical, moderately conformist, that represented a projection of Butler's own character. It is Overton who speaks all the *gnomic* passages in the book. In spite of the savagery of many of them – when he was attacking fathers and father-figures Butler could be brutal – and in spite of the impression conveyed by the book of a frontal attack on all the major Victorian institutions, the novel's message is far from clear-cut and sometimes self-contradictory. The early chapters describing the ancestry of Ernest's father Theobald suggest that heredity is a basic factor in determining character, and sometimes Butler talks as though it is all a matter of evolution, for which no individual can himself be praised or blamed. At other moments he indicates that environment is of the greatest importance, but its relation to innate character is left obscure.

'Being kindly treated at home, he was as fond of his father and mother as it was in his nature to be of anyone, but he was fond of no one else.' This is George Pontifex, Ernest's grandfather, who 'got the greater part of his nature from this obstinate old lady, his mother'. It is in discussing George's nature that Butler is led to reflect on heredity and environment, but to no very distinct purpose. 'Perhaps some men are independent of antecedents and surroundings and have an initial force within themselves which is in no way due to causation: but this is supposed to be a difficult question and it may be as well to avoid it.' More directly related to Butler's views of evolution, which were Lamarckian and anti-Darwinian and from which Bernard Shaw derived *his* views on evolution, is the following passage:

> It would almost seem as if a transmitted education of some generations is necessary for the due enjoyment of great wealth. Adversity, if a man is set down to it by degrees, is more supportable with equanimity by most people than any great prosperity arrived at in a single lifetime. Nevertheless a certain kind of good fortune generally attends self-made men to the last. It is their children of the first, or first and second, generation who are in greater danger, for the race can no more repeat its more successful performances suddenly and without its ebbings and flowings of success than the individual can do so, and the more brilliant the success in any one generation, the greater as a general rule the subsequent exhaustion until time has been allowed for recovery. Hence it often happens that the grandson of a successful man will be more successful than the son. . . . A very successful man, moreover, has something of the hybrid in him; he is a new animal arising

> from the coming together of many unfamiliar elements and it is well known that the reproduction of abnormal growths, whether animal or vegetable, is irregular and not to be depended upon, even when they are not absolutely sterile.

But *The Way of All Flesh* is not a novel about evolution or even about heredity, though heredity figures largely in the early chapters. Once Theobald Pontifex comes to the front of the stage, Butler forgets that he is the product of heredity and environment and proceeds to concentrate on him all his venom. It is strange how suddenly Theobald changes from victim to villain. In the early chapters, he is seen as the product of sadistic paternal domination, even though we are allowed occasionally to see a quite unexplained glimpse of innate vice in him, as in chapter III where we are told that 'Theobald one day beat his nurse and teased her, and when she said she should go away cried out, "You shan't go away – I'll keep you on purpose to torment you",' our sympathy is still largely with him and against his father. He is reduced to a pathetic passive object when the Misses Allaby play at cards for him, and he is trapped into marriage by the winner. And though the Misses Allaby themselves are shown in a most unsympathetic light, Butler goes out of his way to show the economic compulsion under which the Allaby family acted:

> Reader, did you ever have an income at best none too large, which died with you all except £200 a year? Did you ever at the same time have two sons who must be started in life somehow, and five daughters still unmarried

> for whom you would only be too thankful to find husbands – if you knew how to find them? If morality is that which, on the whole, brings a man peace in his declining years – if, that is to say, it is not an utter swindle, can you under these circumstances flatter yourself that you have led a moral life?

Now the point that Butler is making here is precisely the point that underlies most of Jane Austen's novels: the plight of the Allabys is exactly that of the Bennet family in *Pride and Prejudice*. Jane Austen had at least as clear-eyed an awareness of the economic basis of marriage and of the problems of well-bred girls of limited means as Butler had. But she never found it necessary to emerge from behind her characters and speak out in her own person as Butler does. *The Way of All Flesh* is a remarkable document, illustrating a great deal about Victorian *mores* and about Butler's own problems and obsessions, but its grave limitations as a novel are brought sharply into the light when we compare Butler's treatment of the plight of the genteel unmarried female with Jane Austen's.

It is difficult both to explain your characters and to satirize them, and Butler wants to do both. Every now and again he switches off his indignation and turns on the explanation. Some of his explanations seem very odd:

> I grant that at first sight it seems very unjust, that the parents should have the fun and the children be punished for it, but young people should remember that for many years they were part and parcel of their parents and therefore had a good deal of the fun in the person of their

parents. If they have forgotten the fun now, that is no more than people do who have a headache after having been tipsy overnight. The man with a headache does not pretend to be a different person from the man who got drunk, and claim that it is his self of the preceding night and not his self of the morning who should be punished; no more should offspring complain of the headache which it has earned when in the person of its parents, for the continuation of identity, though not so immediately apparent, is just as real in one case as in the other.

It is hard to reconcile this kind of argument with the frontal attack on Victorian parental behaviour which follows soon after:

To parents who wish to lead a quiet life I would say: Tell your children that they are very naughty – much naughtier than most children. Point to the young people of some acquaintances as models of perfection and impress your own children with a deep sense of their own inferiority. You carry so many more guns than they do that they cannot fight you. That is called moral influence, and it will enable you to bounce them as much as you please. They think you know and they will not have yet caught you lying often enough to suspect that you are not the unworldly and scrupulously truthful person which you represent yourself to be: nor yet will they know how great a coward you are, nor how soon you will run away, if they fight you with persistency and judgment. You keep the dice and throw them both for your children and yourself. Load them then, for you can easily manage to stop your children from examining them. . . . True, your children will probably find out all about it some day, but not until too late to be of much service to them or inconvenience to yourself.

Theobald Pontifex is explicitly stated to have behaved in just this manner towards his children. Again and again he is shown as a sadistic monster. ('After some years have gone by he hears his children at their lessons, and the daily oft-repeated screams that issue from the study during the lesson hours tell their own horrible story over the house.') Long after Ernest had emancipated himself from his father, we are told that 'it had been a bitter pill to Theobald to lose his power of plaguing his first-born'. Yet intermittently throughout the novel the whole basis of Butler's moral disapproval of Theobald is slipped from under the reader. Looking back in wealth and emancipation on his earlier days, Ernest told Overton: 'If I had to be born again I would be born at Battersby of the same father and mother as before, and I would not alter anything that has ever happened to me.' And Butler himself endorses this: it all worked out right in the end. In any case, everybody in the novel was caught up in an inevitable chain of cause and effect. At one point Butler actually excuses and pities his villains, Theobald and his wife Christina. After saying that he would have liked to sentence the pair to even greater mental suffering than their son's behaviour actually caused them, he changes his tune:

> But on the other hand, when I thought of Theobald's own childhood, of that dreadful old George Pontifex his father, of John and Mrs John, and of his two sisters, when again I thought of Christina's long years of hope deferred that maketh the heart sick, before she was married, of the life she must have led at Crampsford, and of the surroundings in the midst of which she and her

husband both lived at Battersby, I felt as though the wonder was that misfortunes so persistent had not been followed by even greater retribution.

> Poor people! . . . Who could blame them? They had chapter and verse for everything they had either done or left undone; . . . In what respect had they differed from their neighbours? . . .

It is worth noting that Theobald's father is here called 'that dreadful old George Pontifex', yet in an earlier chapter, in which his death is recounted, Butler goes out of his way to insist that, since virtue consists in being in harmony with one's surroundings, and since George Pontifex 'lived to be nearly seventy-three years old and died rich he must have been in very fair harmony with his surroundings', then his life cannot have been bad. 'Goodness is naught unless it tends towards old age and sufficiency of means.' So George Pontifex must have been good. As for his bad treatment of his children, 'I submit it as the result of my own poor observation, that a good deal of unkindness and selfishness on the part of parents towards children is not generally followed by ill consequences to the parents themselves. They may cast a gloom over their children's lives for many years without having to suffer anything that will hurt them. I should say, then, that it shows no great moral obliquity on the part of parents if within certain limits they make their children's lives a burden to them.' What, then, becomes of Butler's attack on the Victorian family?

The fact is that Butler, in expressly repudiating the evangelical tradition of earnest struggle as a moral criterion, and throwing himself open both to a determinist evolutionary theory of human behaviour on the one hand and a hedonistic theory of value on the other, got himself into a position where he could not logically attack anybody. Indeed, at one point he almost says that if Theobald enjoyed savaging his children, then it was good for him to do so. Yet he was obsessed with the cruelties of his own family life and with the savage vendetta he carried on against his own father. 'Those who have never had a father,' wrote Butler in his *Notebooks*, 'can at any rate never know the sweets of losing one. To most men the death of his father is a new lease of life.' This is more than a Wildean paradox: it is the statement of a personal obsession. This obsession led him to attack father-figures wherever they appeared – not only parents and schoolmasters, but even the great masters in art, music and literature. Italian Renaissance painters, Shakespeare, Milton, Beethoven – any figure esteemed by the Establishment had to be sneered at or at least depreciated in some way. This habit of 'knocking' the established great figures in the arts was revived in our own time by Kingsley Amis, as a sort of parlour game. It is the symptom of the coexistence within a single mind of a variety of new ideas which have iconoclastic implications without adding up to a logically consistent position.

Loss of faith did not then produce in Butler either self-indulgent melancholy or stoic activism. He managed to subsume the religious question in the question of adaptation. One should be a lukewarm Christian, as a matter of social ease. The redeemed and civilized Ernest is made to say in one of his essays: 'We should be churchmen, but somewhat lukewarm churchmen, inasmuch as those who care very much about either religion or irreligion are seldom observed to be very well bred or agreeable people. The Church herself should approach as nearly to that of Laodicea as was compatible with her continuing to be a Church at all, and each individual member should only be hot in striving to be as lukewarm as possible.' And again: 'That a man should have been bred well and breed others well; that his figure, head, hands, feet, voice, manner and clothes should carry conviction upon this point, so that no one can look at him without seeing that he has come of good stock and is likely to throw good stock himself, this is the *desiderandum.*' Ernest inherits a fortune; he never marries (after the collapse of his first marriage which proved not to be a legal marriage after all); his two children are sent away to be brought up by others. This *Bildungsroman* thus ends with the hero educated by life and luck to be a self-indulgent moral and intellectual dandy. This is at the farthest possible remove from the strenuousness of the Victorian prophets, Carlyle, Ruskin, William Morris. With respect to George Eliot's trilogy of God, Immortality, Duty, Butler said through Ernest Pontifex that we assume a half-belief in the first two as a helpful social pose, while the third is something we owe only to ourselves.

The Way of All Flesh is often read by students as the great anti-Victorian novel, a picture of Victorian institutions by a Victorian who anticipated the twentieth-century view of them. But in fact Butler's picture of Victorian institutions is highly eccentric, deeply coloured by his personal obsessions; and his position in attacking them is both confused and highly individual, not at all a position which has been endorsed by any significant twentieth-century writer. True, Bernard Shaw admired Butler enormously and learned from him. But Shaw's exposure of the stupidities and inconsistencies embedded in society was the work of a zealous reformer who really wanted to use his art in order to help change the world. Though he shared some of Butler's views about money and about evolution, the basic pattern of his mind was much further away from Butler's than he appears to have thought. Butler himself disliked Shaw. 'I have long been repelled by this man,' he wrote in his *Notebooks*, 'though at the same time attracted by his coruscating power . . . there is something uncomfortable about the man which makes him uncongenial to me.' Still, there is something Shavian as well as Wildean in many of Butler's witticisms (though some of the most iconoclastic he never had the courage to publish during his lifetime, any more than he did *The Way of All Flesh*). There is a very Shavian ring, for example, about this remark on the Bible in the *Notebooks*:

> *The Song of Solomon* and the book of *Esther* are the most interesting in the old testament, but these are the very ones that make the smallest pretension to holiness, and even these are neither of them of very transcendent merit. They would stand no chance of being accepted by Messrs Cassell and Co., or by any biblical publisher of the present day. Chatto and Windus might take the *Song of Solomon*, but with this exception I doubt if there is a publisher in London who would give a guinea for the pair.

This piece of establishment-knocking comes, significantly, from a passage on Matthew Arnold in which Butler registers his disagreement with Arnold's view that Hebraism, even though it needs to be balanced by Hellenism, still has something valuable to offer us. Butler had been too scarred by the seamier side of the evangelical tradition to feel able to concede this. 'I do not think [Arnold] will get anything from Jerusalem which he will not find better and more easily elsewhere.' So much for moral earnestness. Butler's anti-Puritanism was even stronger than that of the aesthetes. Scepticism made him neither sad nor stoical, but wittily malicious, deliberately outrageous, and a trifle confused.

It would be an over-simplification to say that scepticism plus nonconformist conscience equals stoicism, and scepticism minus nonconformist conscience equals wit, but it does seem to be a fact that only those late Victorian sceptics who either totally abandoned or who had never inherited the nonconformist conscience were able to use their scepticism gaily. Wilde, Shaw and Butler, whatever their differences, had an iconoclastic intellectual gaiety which is quite different from anything to be found in George Eliot, or the Victorian prophets from Carlyle to William Morris, or in Kipling or Housman or Hardy. Shaw, it is true, had his own kind of prophetic earnestness and his own kind of puritanism, but it does not seem to have owed anything to the English evangelical tradition. I have sometimes wondered whether T. S. Eliot's classic diagnosis of 'dissociation of sensibility' might not be applied to this question of scepticism. Eliot saw wit and passion going off in different directions after the end of the seventeenth century, so that serious poetry became solemn and wit was reserved for comic poetry. Intellectual gaiety, which in Shakespeare and Donne could coexist with the deepest seriousness, so that even puns had a place in tragedy, came to be considered incompatible with high seriousness. It might be argued that something similar happened to English intellectual attitudes in general, although the movement was somewhat later than that diagnosed by Eliot. Scepticism was often both elegant and witty in the eighteenth century; it tended to be troubled and solemn in the nineteenth. Only at the end of the century, and even then with not more than a handful of writers, was a re-association of scepticism and intellectual gaiety achieved. But we must make distinctions. Optimistic belief in human rationality could produce a scepticism about traditional creeds, so that certain kinds of eighteenth-century scepticism were not true scepticism but only scepticism with reference to particular dogmas. Hume, who was a true sceptic so far as his view of the limits of rationality was concerned, was far from sceptical about trusting human nature: 'reason is, *and ought to be*, the slave of the passions'. In this respect Butler was more like Hume. The creed that emerges from *The Way of All Flesh* is one of mild and friendly conformity with current prejudice for the sake of a quiet life: Hume would have understood. Shaw's scepticism was scepticism with respect to established Victorian thought but not about the potentiality of human reason in general: in this respect he was more like Voltaire than Hume. His mind was really very much that of the Enlightenment. At bottom he was a utopian rationalist, and used his wit, as Voltaire did, to expose the inconsistencies, confusions, and immoralities of accepted attitudes. Wilde's mind was different again: his tendency was to reduce civilization to a form of play and then cultivate the appropriate gamesmanship.

So long as the sceptic believed that human credulity and human folly were responsible for the dogmatisms and superstitions of the past, he could rejoice in his freedom from the bondage of belief. That was the attitude of the Enlightenment. But, as we have seen, the strong hold of evangelical attitudes that developed in the late eighteenth and early nineteenth centuries prevented many sensitive Victorians from responding cheerfully to their dwindling of belief. They worried about it, as Tennyson and Arnold and Clough did, or they combined their scepticism with moral earnestness or stoic activism, as Henley and Housman and others did. But what of those for whom the universe's new look provided by modern science (especially biology) showed its laws as positively cruel? Tennyson had worried about 'nature red in tooth and claw'. Thomas Hardy, as an old man of eighty, protested when his wife spoke of a 'lovely, frosty morning'. 'It is too inconsiderate of the birds' suffering,' he said. Was he remembering that passage from *The Origin of Species* which he had read in his twenties? 'We behold the face of nature bright with gladness, we often see superabundance of food; we do not see, or we forget, that the birds which are idly singing round us live mostly on insects or seeds, and are thus constantly destroying life; or we forget how largely these songsters, or their eggs, or their nestlings, are destroyed by birds and beasts of prey.'

Hardy's scepticism went deeper than that of any writer I have so far discussed because it involved something more than the absence of an omnipotent and benevolent governor of the universe: it involved the suffering that seemed inherent in the combination of chance, natural law, and environment operating in human affairs. Though there was a stoic element in the creed that Hardy developed, and he admired endurance as much as anything, he was never content to say with Housman that he did not know how the universe was governed but nevertheless knew the necessity for strenuous effort. The disparity between human ambition and the human lot, between the expectations set up by man's make-up and what he was likely to receive in life, strike him as (in the modern existentialist term) absurd. It is not fair that a being constituted as he is should be fated to lead his life in a universe constituted as it is. As a young man of thirty he once jotted in his notebook: 'Mother's notion (and also mine) – that a figure stands in our van with arm uplifted, to knock us back from any pleasant prospect we indulge in as probable.' It is not that Hardy consistently maintened this view, but that the human situation of which this view would seem a rational explanation continually tormented him. Hardy's novels and poems do not project a consistent philosophy, but they do project a consistent view of the human situation and the problems deriving from it that required an answer, whatever answer that was to be. Many of his explanations are tentative: it is as *though* we were dogged by a sardonic fate, governed by a blind doomster, tortured by a sadistic President of the Immortals, worked on by a universal Will struggling to become conscious. So often in his poetry we see the tentative nature of the explanation:

> Has some Vast Imbecility,
> Mighty to build and blend,
> But impotent to tend,
> Framed us in jest, and left us now to hazardry?
> (*Nature's Questioning*)

The burden of Hardy's complaint against the way things were run is less that malevolence is involved than that nothing rational seems to be involved at all. 'The world does not despise us; it only neglects us,' he wrote in his diary in 1865: it is the *indifference* of fate that makes a mockery of man's conviction that he is born to a high destiny or at least to a fate which bears some relation to his desires and hopes. As he pondered over Nature, Chance and Circumstance and acted out in his poems and novels different (yet always related) explanations of this disparity between man's human needs and his actual place in the universe, a view of human life emerges which stands strikingly aloof from that of any other important English writer of his time. We know of course that Hardy was influenced by John Stuart Mill, Herbert Spencer, Leslie Stephen and (though this has been debated) by Schopenhauer, yet his mature views are not to be equated with those of any of these thinkers. Both his scepticism and his pessimism are of a very special kind. (I deliberately call Hardy a pessimist, though I know that at times he rejected the description, that he later considered himself a 'meliorist', and that some critics of Hardy deny or at least qualify his pessimism. I shall come back to this point later, but at this stage wish merely to remark that nobody who comes from a spell of reading in Hardy's poetry and fiction can have the slightest doubt that he has been living with a deeply pessimistic imagination. No amount of analysis in the study can alter this central fact.) His scepticism was not so much a response to intellectual arguments as a response to his experience, and his pessimism was not so much a result of his scepticism as an inference from the nature of the human predicament as he observed and brooded over it. At times, particularly in his earlier years, he seemed to wish that he could resolve the problems that his confrontation of the human lot posed for him by simple belief that somehow, somewhere, a divine providence was working everything out for the best:

> I am like a gazer who should mark
> An inland company
> Standing upfingered, with, 'Hark! hark!
> The glorious distant sea!'
> And feel, 'Alas, 'tis but yon dark
> And wind-swept pine to me!'
>
> Yet I would bear my shortcomings
> With meet tranquillity,
> But for the charge that blessed things
> I'd liefer not have be.

O, doth a bird deprived of wings
Go earth-bound wilfully!
(*The Impercipient*)

Yet Hardy did not agonize over his unbelief, as so many Victorians did: he agonized over the facts of human experience. Even if he had religious belief, it could have coexisted with a profound pessimism about the circumstances of human life on earth. After all, it was a devout Christian who wrote 'Human life is everywhere a state, in which much is to be endured, and little to be enjoyed'. It was that same devout Christian who expressed a most Hardyesque sense of the disparity between what man's make-up conditions him to want and what man's destiny enables him to get: 'What makes the difference between man and all the rest of the animal creation? Every beast, that strays beside me, has the same corporal necessities with myself: he is hungry, and crops the grass, he is thirsty, and drinks the stream, his thirst and hunger are appeased, he is satisfied and sleeps: he rises again and is hungry, he is again fed, and is at rest. I am hungry and thirsty, like him, but when thirst and hunger cease, I am not at rest; I am, like him, pained with want, but am not, like him, satisfied with fullness . . . I can discover within me no power of perception, that is not glutted with its proper pleasure, yet I do not feel myself delighted. Man surely has some latent sense, for which this place affords no gratification; or he has some desires, distinct from sense, which must be satisfied, before he can be happy.' And it was this same devout Christian who savagely mocked an optimistic writer who had suggested an analogy between the human treatment of animals for food and diversion and the treatment of men by superior beings, by taking the analogy further:

> I cannot resist the temptation of contemplating this analogy, which, I think, he might have carried further, very much to the advantage of his argument. He might have shown, that these 'hunters, whose game is man', have many sports analogous to our own. As we drown whelps and kittens, they amuse themselves, now and then, with sinking of a ship, and stand round the fields of Blenheim, or the walls of Prague, as we encircle a cockpit. As we shoot a bird flying, they take a man in the midst of his business or pleasure, and knock him down with an apoplexy. Some of them, perhaps, are virtuosi, and delight in the operations of an asthma as a human philosopher in the effects of an air-pump. To swell a man with a tympany is as good sport as to blow a frog. Many a merry bout have these frolick beings at the vicissitudes of an ague, and good sport it is to see a man tumble with an epilepsy, and revive and tumble again, and all this he knows not why. As they are wiser and more powerful than we, they have more exquisite diversions; for we have no way of procuring any sport so brisk and so lasting, as the paroxysms of the gout and stone, which, undoubtedly, must make high mirth, especially if the play be a little diversified with the blunders and puzzles of the blind and deaf. We know not how far their sphere of observation may extend. Perhaps, now and then, a merry being may place himself in such a situation, as to enjoy, at once, all the varieties of an epidemical disease, or amuse his leisure with the tossing and contortions of every possible pain, exhibited together.

Beside this, Hardy's famous (or notorious) ' "Justice" was done, and the President of the Immortals, in Aeschylean phrase, had ended his sport with Tess' is pretty tame. Yet the devout Christian I have been quoting – who was, of course, Dr Johnson – could agree that human life could logically and plausibly be described as the invention of sadistic gods, holding that Christian faith alone prevented one from believing that it was in fact so. Johnson's reading of the human situation, taken by itself, was not unlike Hardy's – which leads one to wonder how far a man's deepest attitudes are related to the spirit of the age and how far they are essentially a matter of individual temperament. The point I want to emphasize is that it was not scepticism that made Hardy pessimistic; it was his reading of the human situation, a reading which could logically have coexisted, as it did in the case of Dr Johnson, with a religious belief that all would be made good in another world. How, we may ask, did Hardy come to read the situation in the way he did?

We cannot, of course, put it all down to temperament – if only because if we did so there would be nothing more to say. Hardy *was* influenced by Darwin and Mill and Spencer and others. He was aware of the crisis of modern thought that developed particularly in the 1860's, when he was in his twenties. It is true, too, that in his youth he was religious and actually thought of entering the church. He was well on in his twenties when he lost his Christian faith. Yet it was the human condition not the possibility of faith that engaged his real attention. It was as though he said: 'Never mind about Arnold's Sea of Faith retreating: what about the paradoxes, ironies, frustrations and contradictions in the lives of ordinary people?' He changed the terms of the question, which was no more either 'What can I believe?' or even 'What should I do?' but 'What are the true conditions of ordinary human existence?'

This puts Hardy in some degree in the ranks of the social reformers, or at least among those who worried about the 'condition of England question'. Yet Hardy does not emerge primarily as a social reformer or even as a social diagnostician. It is true that his first, unpublished novel, *The Poor Man and the Lady*, was filled with a sense of the burning injustice of the English class system. *The Hand of Ethelberta* contains in its basic plot pattern a strong protest against social snobbery. And there are strong criticisms of English social institutions in all his later fiction, notably in *Tess* and *Jude*. Further, he told William Archer that 'whatever may be the inherent good or evil of life, it is certain that men make it much worse than it need be. When we have got rid of a thousand remediable ills, it will be time enough to determine whether the ill that is irremediable outweighs the good'. And again, he gives evidence in his later work of believing in reform and progress. 'When people of a later age look back upon the barbarous customs and superstitions of the times that we have the unhappiness to live in, what will they say?' Sue Bridehead exclaims to Jude. And the dying Jude reflects that 'our ideas were fifty years too soon to be any good to us'. We may cite, too, the lines he wrote for Miss Ada Rehan to speak at a performance at the

Lyceum Theatre in 1890 in aid of a Holiday Fund for City Children:

> Why should Man add to Nature's quandary,
> And worsen ill . . . ?

Clearly Hardy believed that we must do what we can to lessen remediable social evils: those from Nature are bad enough – why should we add more? Nevertheless, he really believed with Johnson that 'the cure for the greatest part of human miseries is not radical, but palliative'. And even though he eventually worked out an evolutionary position which enabled him to look forward to the time when

> Consciousness the Will informing
> It will fashion all things fair,

the deepest movement of his imagination was backwards, not forwards, and his most characteristic mood was not utopian visioning but nostalgia. Douglas Brown, in his brief but important study of Hardy,[1] attributes this nostalgia to the effects of the agricultural depression which hit England in the 1870's and to the general decline of British agriculture that continued, with a brief rally in the early 1890's, until 1914. The expansion westward of American railroads, the development of cheap ocean-going steamer transport, and the development of agricultural machinery on the American prairies, combined to make imported American wheat much

[1] Douglas Brown: *Thomas Hardy*. London, 1954.

cheaper than that locally produced, and with the repeal of the Corn Laws there remained no obstacle to the importation of grain, so that British farming was faced with steadily increasing foreign competition. Over a million and a half acres of British wheat-fields went out of cultivation between 1870 and 1900. Farmers were ruined; farm labourers flocked to the cities looking for jobs that were often unavailable; the traditional patterns of rural life crumbled so that to physical dereliction was added demoralization and bewilderment. Brown cites Hardy's article, 'The Dorsetshire Labourer', written for *Longman's Magazine* in 1883, when the agricultural depression was acute, and showing a keen perception of the problems of the agricultural worker. This article was quoted by Rider Haggard in his two-volume study of *Rural England*, published in 1902, a study on which Brown draws for lively evidence of the decline of the English countryside. This decline, and the accompanying decline in the rhythms of agricultural life and labour, he sees as the underlying cause of Hardy's pessimism and his nostalgia. It is this decline which, according to Brown, invites the urban invasion of rural areas which further corrupts rural ways of behaving and thinking and also strengthens the temptations of urban life for country dwellers.

Taking *Far From the Madding Crowd*, *The Return of the Native*, *The Woodlanders*, *The Mayor of Casterbridge*, and *Tess of the D'Urbervilles* as Hardy's five great novels (with *Under the Greenwood Tree* as 'fitting prelude' and *Jude the Obscure* as 'impressive epilogue'), Brown traces a common pattern:

> Hardy presents his conception through the play of life in a tract of the countryside. His protagonists are strong-natured countrymen, disciplined by the necessities of agricultural life. He brings into relation with them men and women from outside the rural world, better educated, superior in status, yet inferior in human worth. The contact occasions a sense of invasion, of disturbance. The story unfolds slowly, and the theme of urban invasion declares itself more clearly as the country, its labour, its people and its past consolidate their presence. Then the story assumes some form of dramatic conflict, strong and unsubtle, and the invasion wreaks its havoc. Human relations and human persons are represented less for their own sakes than for the clearer focusing of the invasion and the havoc. A period of ominous waiting may follow; what the situation means becomes more evident: it is a clash between agricultural and urban modes of life. From that point the story moves to its conclusion.

Brown's thesis is sensitively and persuasively presented, yet he never really links up in any inevitable relationship agricultural depression on the one hand and the theme of rural invasion on the other. (The latter, after all, is found also in *Mansfield Park.*) Nor can Hardy's nostalgia be specifically related to what happened to agriculture from the 1870's – a decade, it should be remembered, when Hardy was already in his thirties and had already developed most of his main attitudes. Further, the period of the principal action in *The Mayor of Casterbridge* is 1846 to 1849, nearly thirty years before the great agricultural depression; yet in this novel more, perhaps, than in any other Hardy develops the theme of the decline of the old ways and inruption on the traditional rural scene of new men and new techniques. Certainly, the quarrel between Farfrae and Henshard had nothing to do with the depression of the 1870's and Henshard himself represents an older, pre-rational mode of working with nature, which in its strength and its weakness had deeper implications than can be inferred from the agricultural economics of the time of Hardy's maturity. This is not to say that the plight of British – and more specifically Dorsetshire – agriculture did not work on Hardy's imagination as he wrote his Wessex novels. But it is significant that change in rustic patterns of life and the challenge – or the seduction – presented by the outside world to the closed traditional world of the English rustic are treated by Hardy for the most part in a period deliberately chosen as earlier than his own time. Carl Weber has worked out the dates for the action of each of the novels. *Under the Greenwood Tree* is set in 1835–36; *The Return of the Native* in 1842–43; *The Mayor of Casterbridge*, as I have noted, in 1846–49. Why did Hardy set these novels so early if he was concerned primarily with what the agricultural depression of the 1870's had done to rural English life? For it must be stressed that the sense of change and the theme of intrusion are central to these novels at least as much as to those set in later periods. *The Woodlanders* is set in 1876–79, squarely in the period of agricultural depression; yet its theme of the conflict of older, deeper rhythms of rustic life with the newer, shallower currents coming in from outside owes nothing to the economic plight of arable farming at the time. Only in *Tess* set in 1884–89, do we find a sense of economic change in contemporary agricultural life linked to the main action of the novel.

One can concede all this, yet still say with Brown that Hardy's imagination was moved to take the direction it did by his response to the plight of the countryside from the 1870's; it is certainly significant that his novels begin to appear in the 70's. But the sources of Hardy's nostalgia seem to run deeper than this. Brown himself has an interesting passage in this connexion:

> The earlier novels celebrate rural manners and values; they work through deep but simple natures to establish respect for human dignity rather than human complexity. Their fables neglect the family, and the breeding and rearing of children, as if from Hardy's inner powerlessness to envisage a future as warmly and generously as he envisages the past.

Only when he comes to *Jude*, his last novel, Brown goes on to observe, does Hardy move to more complex worlds. This novel 'takes the gifted and ambitious villager into the civic world, a milieu of intellect, introspection and subtle self-consciousness. It works through natures far from simple, and its fable concerns itself (to painful effect) with responsible married life, and the breeding of children'.

This is justly said. But why, it might be asked, does Hardy seem at his most defeatist when dealing with the more complex problems of adjustment and relationships in the modern world? In his 1895 preface to *Jude* Hardy said that his intention in writing the novel was 'to tell, without a mincing of words, of a deadly war waged between flesh and spirit'. It was 'a tragedy of unfulfilled aims'. And certainly the question of reform of the marriage laws and the widening of educational opportunity – on both of which topics he touched in his preface of 1912 – had nothing to do with the plight of British agriculture. Yet in this very preface Hardy conceded that 'no doubt there can be more in a book than the author consciously puts there'. For all the implied pleas for reform in *Jude* it is not a reformist novel but a fatalistic one. Its theme was the theme expressed by Fulke Greville and quoted by Aldous Huxley:

> Oh, wearisome condition of humanity!
> Born under one law, to another bound.

Self-consciousness complicates and deepens the problem – which is surely one reason for Hardy's nostalgia for the older rhythms of rustic life, when traditional ways of acting and feeling were more or less automatic. It is a rootedness in such traditional ways that enables Hardy's tragic rustics (like Marty South in *The Woodlanders*) to endure. This clashes oddly with Hardy's later view that the Immanent Will was becoming conscious and that this might improve the way the universe was run. I cannot feel that Hardy's deepest kinds of awareness were involved in this formulation. The disparity between man's nature and his destiny and the basic fact of man's subjection to time were his true themes, though of course in different novels he plays all sorts of variation on them. None of the ironies of fate can compare with the fundamental ironies of nature's inability to satisfy the psychological needs with which she has endowed man and man's vulnerability to time and change. True, we come close to an important source of Hardy's thought and feeling when we read what he has to say about the decline of the countryside in his essay on 'The Dorsetshire Labourer'. But do we not get closer still when we read his poem *During Wind and Rain*?

They sing their dearest songs –
He, she, all of them – yea,
Treble and tenor and bass,
  And one to play;
With the candles mooning each face. . . .
  Ah, no; the years O!
How the sick leaves reel down in throngs!

They clear the creeping moss –
Elders and juniors – aye,
Making the pathways neat
  And the garden gay;
And they build a shady seat. . . .
  Ah, no; the years, the years;
See, the white storm-birds wing across!

They are blithely breakfasting all –
Men and maidens – yea,
Under the summer tree,
  With a glimpse of the bay,
While pet fowl come to the knee. . . .
  Ah, no; the years O!
And the rotten rose is ript from the wall.

They change to a high new house,
He, she, all of them – aye,
Clocks and carpets and chairs
  On the lawn all day,
And brightest things that are theirs. . . .
  Ah, no; the years, the years;
Down their carved names the rain-drop ploughs.

Modern scholarship has identified the precise moments in Hardy's life that are recollected here. But that is of little importance. The poem carries its own intense and moving conviction. This is on an altogether different plane from the self-indulgent and languid moaning of Ernest Dowson and the aesthetes; it is, too, more real and more shot through with a sense of felt life than the stoic gestures of Housman or even the beautifully cadenced melancholy of Tennyson. The sadness in this poem is not a pose; it has nothing to do with problems of faith or unbelief or with the question of the age of the world or the descent of man. It arises from the deepest level of experience, and also from the simplest and most elemental. And surely this poem explains as well as anything can explain what Brown called 'Hardy's inner powerlessness to envisage a future as warmly and generously as he envisages the past'.

The paradox about Hardy is that while he is one of the most local of our writers – after all, Hardy's Wessex must be about the best known area of England among readers of English literature wherever they live – he really requires least local explanation. Hardy's pessimism – his sadness, if you prefer, as I do, to call it that – has a more elemental quality about it than that of any other writer I have so far discussed. And while I do not wish to get into any argument about nature versus nurture as determining factors in the attitudes of writers, I must register my opinion that, in any discussion of Victorian doubt, scepticism, stoicism, pessimism, and related attitudes, when you come to Hardy you are given pause. One does not really want to choose between, say, Harvey Webster's account of the development of Hardy's thought in terms of ideas and intellectual influences and Douglas Brown's account in terms of the plight of the English peasantry. Both are helpful, yet both obscure in some degree an important truth. Hardy had a tragic temperament and in his finest work he carries deep into the reader's consciousness his sense of the built-in causes for sadness in the human condition. In his best poetry, which is some of the finest in the English language and arguably greater than any of his novels, in spite of the apparent hit-or-miss quality of the language, the mixing of archaic poetic forms with modern colloquialisms, and all sorts of other theoretical infelicities (infelicities, that is, on a Tennysonian standard), the human voice comes through with haunting precision, reminding us above all of man's subjection to time and change and memory. Without self-pity, without attitudinizing, but by a kind of rapt recording, Hardy tells the truth about what it is to be human. Ever since Eliot insisted on our separating the artist from the sufferer, the craft from the personality, we have been shy of admitting that a voice speaking with an almost trance-like sincerity under the pressure of personal emotion can achieve great poetry. It is disturbing to anyone who has learned from Eliot that 'the difference between art and the event is always absolute' and that 'poetry . . . is not the expression of personality, but an escape from personality' to realize that some of the greatest poetry of modern times was written by Hardy under the direct pressure of his emotions after the death of his first wife. Those poems of 1912 and 1913 are worlds away from the great Victorian elegies, from *In Memoriam* or *Thyrsis*. The quiet voice of a poet who has his eye fixed on an inner memory and who seems to be ignoring the reader, who is not constructing a great artifact as a memorial to the dead but fixing with desperate calm his mood of recollection and regret, speaks for no period mood or spirit of the age. How crudely rhetorical are Henley's boastings from the pit about his unconquerable soul beside *this* desperately human voice:

You did not walk with me
Of late to the hill-top tree
    By the gated ways,
    As in earlier days;
    You were weak and lame,
    So you never came,
And I went alone, and I did not mind.
Not thinking of you as left behind.

I walked up there to-day
Just in the former way;

Surveyed around
The familiar ground
By myself again:
What difference, then?
Only that underlying sense
Of the look of a room on returning thence.

3

> There is not a creed which is not shaken, not an accredited dogma which is not shown to be questionable, not a received tradition which does not threaten to dissolve. Our religion has materialised itself in the fact, in the supposed fact; it has attached its emotion to the fact, and now the fact is failing it. But for poetry the idea is everything; the rest is a world of illusion, of divine illusion. Poetry attaches its emotion to the idea; the idea *is* the fact. The strongest part of our religion to-day is its unconscious poetry.

These famous words of Matthew Arnold, first published in 1879 and quoted again the following year in his introduction to Ward's *English Poets*, represent a classic statement of the way in which a certain sector of what might be called English liberal intellectuals met the threat to fundamentalist Christianity posed by new scientific discoveries and biblical scholarship. When he wrote these words Arnold had already pondered and written much on the question, and provided English liberal theology with its charter. In 1873, in his conclusion to *Literature and Dogma*, he had written:

> Culture, then, and science and literature are requisite, in the interest of religion itself, even when, taking nothing but *conduct* into account, we rightly make the God of the Bible, as Israel made him, to be simply and solely 'the

> Eternal Power, not ourselves, that makes for *righteousness*'. For we are not to forget, that, grand as this conception of God is, and well as it meets the wants of far the largest part of our being, of three-fourths of it, yet there is one-fourth of our being of which it does not strictly meet the wants, the part which is concerned with art and science; or, in other words, with beauty and exact knowledge.
>
> For the total man, therefore, the truer conception of God is as 'the Eternal Power, not ourselves, by which all things fulfil the law of their being'; by which, therefore, we fulfil the law of our being so far as our being is aesthetic and intellective, as well as so far as it is moral.

And two years later, in *God and the Bible*, he concluded:

> We have to renounce impossible attempts to receive the legendary and miraculous matter of Scripture as grave historical and scientific fact. We have to accustom ourselves to regard henceforth all this part as poetry and legend.

In poeticizing the Bible, Arnold transferred to poetry the role hitherto reserved for religion. 'The future of poetry is immense, because in poetry, where it is worthy of its high destinies, our race, as time goes on, will find an ever surer and surer stay.' One might observe that this has proved to be a most erroneous prophecy: poetry is not the main prop and comfort of our population today. But the literary critics have taken from Arnold something of their deep sense of their responsibility to civilization: if poetry (by which Arnold meant imaginative literature in general) is to replace religion as the centre of a culture, then it must have its priests as religion has had; they must establish its canon and teach others how to distinguish the true Word from the false and the heretical. The critic becomes a priestly interpreter of the true Word to the people and a mediator between the poet and his public. The heroic activity of F. R. Leavis in establishing what he called 'The Great Tradition' was the exact equivalent of the establishment of a canon, inwardness with which alone would bring cultural salvation.

But all this really shirks the question of moral absolutes, duty, 'conduct' as Matthew Arnold called it, of which he considered that three-fourths of life consisted. A subtilizing of our awareness through a proper response to imaginative literature does not yield immediate dividends in conduct, if indeed it ever yields them. Neither the most sensitive critics nor the greatest writers are known for their superior moral behaviour, whatever moral standard we take. I don't think that even Dr Leavis (who has become accustomed to the charge of Puritanism so often levelled against him) would consider with Milton that anyone ambitious to be a true poet or critic 'ought himself to be a true poem'. D. H. Lawrence's most fervent admirers do not hold up his personal behaviour as a model, nor do ardent Joyceans recommend that we should imitate in detail Joyce's conduct in his personal life. These are not frivolous points: what I want to draw attention to is the fact that the Victorian crisis of faith concerned the ultimate sanctions for morality and that the interpretation of the Bible as poetry has not helped to solve that problem at all. Perhaps I ought to add that I agree with Arnold that much of the Bible is remarkable poetry, and I read and appreciate it as such. But the ethical problem remains. There were many Victorians who believed that a God who was reduced to an eternal power not ourselves, even if in some highly abstract sense that power 'made for righteousness', could not be a source of moral absolutes. Ivan Karamazov's position that if God did not exist everything was permitted could be extended to the proposition that if God was merely a metaphysician's abstract name for the ultimate forces that govern the universe, and had not personally revealed a code of conduct for man, then, too, everything might be permitted.

As we have seen, the nonconformist conscience survived the theological sanctions on which it was originally based. But there were few nineteenth-century writers who really confronted the paradox involved in this survival. There was one, however, in whom it survived and who worked out a rationale for its survival, a writer who, more than any other in the nineteenth century, confronted both its social problem – the 'condition of England question' – and its crisis of faith with intelligence, humanity, and a moral and intellectual honesty beside which Arnold's poeticizing of the Bible seems intellectual pussyfooting and the thunderings of Carlyle, the prophesyings of Ruskin and the socialist visions of William Morris seem mere rhetoric. Listen to this voice (the subject is the stoic emperor Marcus Antoninus):

> He was in the position in which many of us are now. He had no traditionary faith to which he could resort for oracular and unquestionable replies to all his doubts. The

> old Roman worship had decayed, and whatever help was necessary he had to obtain for himself. It is probable that all men who think at all about these things are compelled to work out their own salvation, even if born into the straitest sect from which they may never stray. Bunyan, for example, although orthodox, could not escape the universal destiny, and had an Apollyonic conflict lasting over years before he found peace. Nevertheless, it ever must be true that, when popular religions have all gone to dust, or when, as in our day, they are half-way towards it – the most disgusting stage of all putrefaction – our difficulties are increased and the solitude is deepened.

This is William Hale White ('Mark Rutherford'), writing in the *Secular Review* in July 1880. And this is how White puts the point that Arnold had made about the need for both the moral and the aesthetic. It is from his book on Bunyan, published in 1904:

> Puritanism has done noble service, but we have seen enough of it even in Bunyan to show that it is not an entirely accurate version of God's message to man. It is the most distinct, energetic, salutary movement in our history, and no other religion has surpassed it in preaching the truths by which men and nations must exist. Nevertheless we need Shakespeare as well as Bunyan, and oscillate between the *Pilgrim's Progress* and *As You Like It*. We cannot bring ourselves into a unity. The time is yet to come when we shall live by a faith which is a harmony of all our faculties.

Now the really interesting thing about William Hale White's praise of Puritanism in this passage is that he had earned the right to praise it. For no man had so devastatingly exposed the narrowness, cruelty, and sometimes even the stupidity and hypocrisy bred by the English evangelical tradition than he had in his best known work, *The Autobiography of Mark Rutherford*. His exposure of the theological teaching at Cheshunt College is all the more powerful for the quiet tone in which it is written:

> Systematic theology was the next science to which the President directed us. We used a sort of Calvinistic manual which began by setting forth that mankind was absolutely in God's power. He was our maker, and we had no legal claim whatever to any consideration from Him. The author then mechanically built up the Calvinistic creed, step by step, like a house of cards. Systematic theology was the great business of our academical life. We had to read sermons to the President in class, and no sermon was considered complete and proper unless it unfolded what was called the scheme of redemption from beginning to end.
>
> So it came to pass that about the Bible . . . we were in darkness. It was a magazine of texts, and those portions of it which contributed nothing in the shape of texts, or formed no part of the scheme, were neglected. Worse still, not a word was ever spoken to us telling us in what manner to strengthen the reason, to subdue the senses, or in what way to deal with all the varied diseases of that soul of man which we were to set ourselves to save. All its failing, infinitely more complicated than those of the body, were grouped as 'sin', and for these there was one quack remedy. If the patient did not like the remedy, or got no good from it, the fault was his.
>
> It is remarkable that the scheme was never of the slightest service to me in repressing one solitary evil

> inclination; at no point did it come into contact with me. At the time it seemed right and proper that I should learn it, and I had no doubt of its efficacy; but when the stress of temptation was upon me, it never occurred to me, nor when I became a minister did I find it sufficiently powerful to mend the most trifling fault. In after years, but not till I had strayed far away from the President and his creed, the Bible was really opened to me, and became to me, what it now is, the most precious of books.

Mark Rutherford's experiences are, of course, William Hale White's. Although he changed a few details, the autobiography is in all essential points wholly accurate and honest – we have only to read through the much later and briefer 'Autobiographical Notes' (published in 1913 as *The Early Life of Mark Rutherford*) to see this at once. *The Autobiography of Mark Rutherford* is of historical importance as the finest and most sensitive account of the Victorian crisis of faith and (in *Mark Rutherford's Deliverance*) its resolution; we see the *process* whose results Arnold describes, and we see it as it operates on the mind and character of a remarkable individual. But White's books are of much more than documentary interest. For his resolution was a highly individual one, and his record of it, and of its consequences for his later thought and imagination as shown in his later novels, constitutes a unique chapter in late nineteenth-century literature. Here we see something of the subtlety and resilience of the nonconformist conscience. It is not just a fact of social history, but a human dilemma working itself out.

Arnold talked about religion and poetry. But 'Mark

Rutherford' remembered and recalled precisely how poetry came to his rescue and rekindled religious feeling within him:

> During the first two years at college my life was entirely external. My heart was altogether untouched by anything I heard, read, or did, although I myself supposed that I took an interest in them. But one day in my third year, a day I remember as well as Paul must have remembered afterwards the day on which he went to Damascus, I happened to find amongst a parcel of books a volume of poems on paper boards. It was called *Lyrical Ballads*, and I read first one and then the whole book. It conveyed to me no new doctrine, and yet the change it wrought in me could only be compared with that which is said to have been wrought on Paul himself by the Divine apparition.
>
> Looking over the *Lyrical Ballads* again, as I have looked over it a dozen times since then, I can hardly see what it was which stirred me so powerfully, nor do I believe that it communicated much to me which could be put in words. But it executed a movement and growth which went on till, by degrees, all the systems which enveloped me like a body gradually decayed from me and fell away into nothing. Of more importance, too, than the decay of systems was the birth of a habit of inner reference and a dislike to occupy myself with anything which did not in some way or other touch the soul, or was not the illustration or embodiment of some spiritual law. . . . Wordsworth unconsciously did for me what every religious reformer has done – he re-created my Supreme Divinity; substituting a new and living spirit for the deity, once alive, but gradually hardened into an idol.

That phrase 'once alive' is important in Hale White's thought, for it reflects his passionate concern with the true sources of religious belief, the needs which such belief arose in order to meet and the way the imagination had worked in producing the belief. It was this that started his trouble with the college authorities which ended in his expulsion:

> Nearly every doctrine in the college creed had once had a natural origin in the necessities of human nature, and might therefore be so interpreted as to become a necessity again. To reach through to that original necessity; to explain the atonement as I believe it appeared to Paul, and the sinfulness of man as it appeared to the prophets, was my object. But it was precisely this reaching after a meaning which constituted heresy. The distinctive essence of our orthodoxy was not this or that dogma, but the acceptance of dogmas as communications from without, and not as born from within.
>
> Heresy began, and in fact was altogether present, when I said to myself that a mere statement of the atonement as taught in class was impossible for me, and that I must go back to Paul and his century, place myself in his position, and connect the atonement through him with something which I felt. I thus continued to use all the terms which I had hitherto used; but an uneasy feeling began to develop itself about me in the minds of the professors, because I did not rest in the 'Simplicity' of the gospel. To me this meant its unintelligibility.

While it is true that William Hale White's unique sensibility and remarkable power of pellucid writing makes Mark Rutherford's case rather special, it is also true that the account of Cheshunt College ('the Countess of Huntingdon's College', which admitted only those that belonged to 'the Connexion', i.e. the evangelical sect of Independents), which is the 'Dissenting College not very far from where we lived', brings home to us, much more vividly that any standard historical account based on the debate as carried on in *Essays and Reviews* and other high levels could possibly do, the mind of the ordinary English Dissenter of the mid nineteenth century. Mark Rutherford's response to that mind was something special in its quality (though not in its general nature): the mind itself as he shows it to us must have been typical of large areas of middle-class Christian thought at the time. It was in fact not from Cheshunt College but from a similar institution, New College, St John's Wood, to which White transferred from Cheshunt in 1851 or 1852, that he was expelled.

The singular honesty of William Hale White's account of the development of his opinions comes through again and again in his willingness to admit inconsistencies and even confusion in his position. In the 'Autobiographical Notes' he adds an interesting footnote to his account of Mark Rutherford's response to Wordsworth:

> On the bookshelf in our dining-room lay a volume of Wordsworth. One day, when I was about eighteen, I took it out, and fell upon the lines –
>
> 'Knowing that Nature never did betray
> The heart that loved her.'
>
> What they meant was not clear to me, but they were a signal of the approach of something which turned out to be of the greatest importance, and altered my history.

'What they meant was not clear to me.' White never

rationalizes after the event. Indeed, in *The Autobiography of Mark Rutherford* he introduces characters whose function is to speak for another side of his own mind and test ironically the strength and consistency of his developing convictions. At the same time he may intervene to speak in his own person – an older man looking back on his youth – in order to set his mature ideas beside the often troubled and confused notions of his younger self. This has the effect of keeping in counterpoint a number of complementary (if not of actually conflicting) ideas. He describes how his friend Edward Gibbon Mardon, the sympathetic but highly critical sceptic, shook his naïve faith in personal immortality:

> In theory I had long despised the notion that we should govern our conduct here by hope of reward or fear of punishment hereafter. But under Mardon's remorseless criticism, when he insisted on asking for the where and how, and pointed out that all attempts to say where and how ended in nonsense, my hope began to fail, and I was surprised to find myself incapable of living with proper serenity if there was nothing but blank darkness before me at the end of a few years.
>
> As I got older I became aware of the folly of this perpetual reaching out after the future, and of drawing from to-morrow, and from to-morrow only, a reason for the joyfulness of to-day. I learned, when, alas! it was almost too late, to live in each moment as it passed over my head, believing that the sun as it is now rising is as good as it will ever be, and blinding myself as much as possible to what may follow. But when I was young I was the victim of that illusion, implanted for some purpose or other in us by Nature, which causes us, on the brightest morning in June, to think immediately of a brighter

> morning which is to come in July. I say nothing, now, for or against the doctrine of immortality. All I say is, that men have been happy without it, even under pressure of disaster, and that to make immortality a sole spring of action here is an exaggeration of the folly which deludes us all through life with endless expectation, and leaves us at death without the thorough enjoyment of a single hour.

So he sets up against the conventional Christian notion of living for the next world his own version of *carpe diem*, almost, we might say, his own version of the Paterian doctrine of savouring all experience to the full; yet it has ethical overtones not normally associated with either of these other two doctrines. There is, as many other passages in his works make clear, a stoic element in his doctrine of making the most of the present: sometimes the present demands mere endurance, and that can be hard enough. At the same time, in the preface to the second edition of the *Autobiography*, supposedly written by the friend who edited Mark Rutherford's papers after his death but of course really representing his own views quite directly, he gives an almost hedonistic twist to the traditional Christian doctrine of remaining content in the station in which you find yourself:

> If we wish to be happy, and have to live as average men and women, as most of us have to live, we must learn to take an interest in the topics which concern average men and women. We think too much of courselves. We ought not to sacrifice a single moment's pleasure in an attempt to do something which is too big for us, and as a rule,

> men and women are always attempting what is too big for them. . . .
>
> It is not only a duty to ourselves, but it is a duty to others to take this course. Great men do the world much good, but not without some harm, and we have no business to be troubling ourselves with their dreams if we have duties which lie nearer home amongst persons to whom these dreams are incomprehensible. Many a man goes into his study, shuts himself up with his poetry or his psychology, comes out, half understanding what he has read, is miserable because he cannot find anybody with whom he can talk about it, and misses altogether the far more genuine joy which he could have obtained from a game with his children or listening to what his wife had to tell him about her neighbours.

This is White's very personal version of the Christian ideal of humility. It reaches out to other currents in Victorian thought, twining together strands of both hedonism and stoicism into a doctrine composed essentially of a revaluation in terms of human psychological needs and ethical demands of traditional Christian thought.

White goes much beyond Arnold in re-defining the nature and purpose of religion, for he was continually coming down to cases and asking in specific detail exactly what need it was that religion served. That is how he managed to relate his discussions of the two great problems of the latter nineteenth century – poverty and the social question on the one hand and the crisis of faith on the other. In *Mark Rutherford's Deliverance* there is a classic description of the horrors and hopelessness of a life of real poverty in a London slum, but it is associated with the question of what sort of doctrine if any can help these people. When Mark Rutherford and his friend M'Kay set out to help the poor of Drury Lane they soon learned their inability to achieve anything on a large scale; but they did help a handful, by simple practical measures. Those measures included acting out, as it were, a state of mind. Religion as normally preached to the hopeless poor was quite useless:

> I do not think that church or chapel would have done them much good. Preachers are like unskilled doctors with the same pill and draught for every complaint. They do not know where the fatal spot lies on lung or heart or nerve which robs us of life. If any of these persons just described had gone to church or chapel they would have heard discourses on the usual set topics, none of which would have concerned them. Their trouble was not the forgiveness of sins, the fallacies of Arianism, the personality of the Holy Ghost, or the doctrine of the Eucharist. They all *wanted* something distinctly. They had great gaping needs which they longed to satisfy, intensely practical and special. Some of these necessities no words could in any way meet.

So Rutherford and M'Kay provide a humble meeting place for those few of the extreme poor whom they were able to make contact with. And this is how he describes their aim:

> What gospel had we to give? Why, in short, did we meet on the Sunday? What was our justification? In the first place, there was the simple quietude. The retreat from the streets and from miserable cares into a place where there was peace and room for reflection was something. It is all very well for cultivated persons with libraries to scoff at

> religious services. To the poor the cathedral or the church might be an immense benefit, if only for the reason that they present a barrier to worldly noise, and are a distinct invitation by architecture and symbolic decoration to meditation on something beyond the business which presses on them during the week. Poor people frequently cannot read for want of a place in which to read. Moreover, they require to be provoked by a stronger stimulus than that of a book.

Even so, Rutherford and M'Kay ministered only to four not wholly desperate cases they had managed to establish contact with. For them, it seemed possible that they might succeed in their aim of creating 'contentment with their lot, and even some joy in it'. 'For,' Mark Rutherford adds, 'that was our religion; that was the central thought of all we said and did, giving shape and tendency to everything.' It might be said that this was a wickedly reactionary activity, trying to reconcile the poor and the oppressed with their lot. But William Hale White knew perfectly well that whatever the long-term plans of reformers, they could not help elderly individuals already battered almost beyond endurance by misfortune. There is a kind of social reformer who welcomes the deepening of social and economic horror as it will increase discontent and alert law-makers to the desperate need for remedies. And there is the revolutionary who welcomes the growth of discontent as furthering the aims of the revolution. But such views are bound to write off the elderly battered sufferer as irredeemable. Reformers and revolutionaries work for the next generation. The individual for whom any political measure will come too late is nevertheless an individual, and it is not necessarily reactionary to try to help him to a more equable state of mind in the midst of his sorry plight. It was his genius for getting down to cases, for testing out his convictions with reference to people as he found them, that makes White's involvement with the social question so interesting. He was not in any sense a 'pie in the sky' man. We have glanced at his attitude to immortality and seen that he did not look there for hope. Nor did he believe that even the most eloquent and beautiful preaching – even that of Jesus himself – would help people fallen below a certain level. After one of the grimmest descriptions of squalid poverty in English literature, he goes on to comment:

> Here was nothing but sullen subjugation, the most grovelling slavery, mitigated only by a tendency to mutiny. Here was a strength of circumstance to quell and dominate which neither Jesus nor Paul could have overcome – worse a thousandfold than Scribes or Pharisees, or any form of persecution. The preaching of Jesus would have been powerless here; in fact, no known stimulus, nothing ever held before men to stir the soul to activity, can do anything in the back streets of great cities so long as they are the cesspools which they now are.

Sometimes White talks almost like a modern existentialist. Man, faced by pain and death, must choose a faith and hold to it. Consider, for example, this passage, also from *Mark Rutherford's Deliverance*:

> Pain and death are nothing new, and men have been

driven into perplexed scepticism and even insurrection by them, ever since men came into being. Always, however, have the majority, the vast majority of the race, felt instinctively that in this scepticism and insurrection they could not abide, and they have struggled more or less blindly after explanation; determined not to desist till they had found it, and reaching a result embodied in a multitude of shapes irrational and absurd to the superficial scoffer, but of profound interest to the thoughtful. I may observe, in passing, that this is a reason why all great religions should be treated with respect, and in a certain sense preserved. It is nothing less than a wicked waste of accumulated human strivings to sneer them out of existence. They will be found, every one of them, to have incarnated certain vital doctrines which it has cost centuries of toil and devotion properly to appreciate. . . . Of one thing I am certain, that their rediscovery and restoration will be necessary. I cannot too earnestly insist upon the need of our holding, each man for himself, by some faith which shall anchor him. It must not be taken up by chance. We must fight for it, for only so will it become *our* faith. The halt in indifference or in hostility is easy enough and seductive enough. The half-hearted thinks that when he has attained that stage he has completed the term of human wisdom. I say go on: do not stay there; do not take it for granted that there is nothing beyond; incessantly attempt an advance, and at last a light, dim it may be, will arise. It will not be a completed system, perfect on all points, an answer to all our questions, but at least it will give ground for hope.

A willed and admittedly partial faith, held to in the clear realization that full knowledge is impossible, is part of White's answer to the crisis of faith of his day. You can build moral absolutes on tentative creeds, he seems to feel, if those creeds are worked out in full awareness of man's basic needs. We can actually see in White's books how a certain kind of scepticism comes to coexist with an imperative sense of duty. With George Eliot we see the coexistence of scepticism and duty working effectively in her novels (the character of Romola, though not her happiest creation, is the clearest embodiment of this coexistence), but we do not see the process which enabled her to reach this solution in her own mind. In *The Autobiography of Mark Rutherford* and *Mark Rutherford's Deliverance* we see the process working itself out. In the later novels we see the end-product of the process being applied.

But before leaving the *Deliverance*, I want to quote from the paragraph which immediately follows on the one just quoted:

> We had to face the trials of our friends, and we had to face death. I do not say for an instant that we had any effectual reply to these great arguments against us. We never so much as sought for one, knowing how all men had sought and failed. But we were able to say there is some compensation, that there is another side, and this is all that man can say. No theory of the world is possible.

'No theory of the world is possible'! We are reminded of Housman's profession of ignorance of how the world is governed. But note how White continues:

> The storm, the rain slowly rotting the harvest, children sickening in cellars are obvious; but equally obvious are an evening in June, the delight of men and women in one another, in music, and in the exercise of thought . . . I may observe, too, that although it is usually supposed, it is

> erroneously supposed, that it is pure doubt which disturbs or depresses us. Simple suspense is in fact very rare, for there are few persons so constituted as to be able to remain in it. It is dogmatism under the cloak of doubt which pulls us down. It is the dogmatism of death, for example, which we have to avoid. The open grave is dogmatic, and we say *that man has gone*, but this is as much a transgression of the limits of certitude as if we were to say *he is an angel in bliss*. The proper attitude, the attitude enjoined by the severest exercise of the reason is, *I do not know*; and in this there is an element of hope, now rising and now falling, but always sufficient to prevent that blank despair which we must feel if we consider it as settled that when we lie down under the grass there is an absolute end.

This is a curious conclusion to follow on from White's earlier statement that we must take up a faith and fight for it. 'The proper attitude . . . is *I do not know*.' And it is this agnosticism that prevents despair. It enables us to enjoy what life offers us that can be enjoyed, and to avoid despair when faced with the death of our friends or with the prospect of our own death. Of course White is inconsistent. Part of the fascination of these books is that one can follow the precise curve of his mind and sensibilities as they respond to different phases of his own experience. It is this that makes so many other Victorian presentations of the crisis of faith either airy or mechanical or superficial or, in a rather dubious sense, 'literary'. Even Gosse's *Father and Son*, a classic of Victorian religious revolt marked by humanity and compassion, shows how biblical fundamentalism frustrated a scientist's development but does not show the son as doing more than move from his father's position into a genial cultural scepticism that simply ceases to confront the psychological and moral problems that the father's religion was designed to solve. Gosse was doing something other than Mark Rutherford, whose main concern was to work out a creed for himself and share it with unknown readers. And always for Rutherford the ethical question was central. Here, in a final quotation from *Mark Rutherford's Deliverance*, is a statement of the position of the late nineteenth-century liberal Christian which yet differs from most other statements of that position in literature in its almost obsessive ethical concern:

> We endeavoured to follow Christianity in the depth of its distinction between right and wrong. Herein this religion is of priceless value. Philosophy proclaims the unity of our nature. To philosophy every passion is as natural as every act of saintlike negation, and one of the usual effects of thinking or philosophising is to bring together all that is apparently contrary in man, and to show how it proceeds really from one centre. But Christianity had not to propound a theory of man; it had to redeem the world. It laid awful stress on the duality in us, and the stress laid on that duality is the world's salvation. The words right and wrong are not felt now as they were felt by Paul. They shade off one into the other. Nevertheless, if mankind is not to be lost, the ancient antagonism must be maintained. The shallowest of mortals is able now to laugh at the notion of a personal devil. No doubt there is no such thing existent; but the horror at evil which could find no other expression than in the creation of a devil is no subject for laughter, and if it does not in some shape or other survive, the race itself will not survive.

Matthew Arnold might have said that the creation of the

devil was an act of the poetic imagination and accepted the devil as a poetic character. But it is White who explains how the poetry works and wherein lies its value. Further, White's linking of this kind of poetry with the profoundest workings of the ethical imagination is a much more concrete operation than Arnold's talk of 'high seriousness' and quotation of touchstone lines. (Perhaps I should add, to avoid misunderstanding, that I am not saying that White is *right* in all that he says. Modern psychology can explain much that White treats as a purely ethical matter. And poetry is more than the projection of an ethical idea by means of a symbolic character. But I *am* saying that White engages with his subject, the nineteenth-century crisis of faith, more impressively than any other Victorian man of letters and, further, that he relates this to the social question in an original and moving way.)

Arnold, it will be remembered, disliked melancholy without action even though his most characteristic poetry ran in that direction. Hale White, in discussing his struggle against what he called 'the terrors of depression' regards the melancholy mood as a kind of sloth. 'There is really more strength of mind required for resolving the commonest difficulty than is necessary for the production of poems on these topics. The characteristic of so much that is said and written now is melancholy; and it is melancholy, not because of any deeper acquaintance with the secrets of man than that which was possessed by our forefathers, but because it is easy to be melancholy, and the time lacks strength.' This is the stoic side of White's thought.

In quoting from *The Autobiography of Mark Rutherford* and *Mark Rutherford's Deliverance* in order to illustrate their author's attitude to religious and social questions I may have given the impression that I regard these works primarily as collections of aphorisms or declarations of belief. If so, I have given a most misleading impression. For these are skilfully constructed novels in which, autobiographical though they are, especially the former, the characters and incidents are related in a most impressive way in order to create a pattern of meaning which goes beyond any quotable 'gnomic' passage. When we look, for example, at the various kinds of marital relationships in these novels, when we see the various ways in which the relation between intelligence and moral behaviour operates in the different characters and their relations with each other, when we note how different kinds of hypocrisy, timidity, self-indulgence, pride, endurance, scepticism, faith, manifest themselves in particular characters at particular crises in the action, we begin to understand that William Hale White invented a new kind of novel, that is a kind of fable that is much richer and more complex than a fable, that is autobiography yet which transcends autobiography, that is a *Bildungsroman* without the obvious schematic development of most examples of that genre, that is a 'novel of ideas' while remaining a quietly honest narrative deeply human in its significance and genuinely moving as a human document.

Of William Hale White's other novels – all written under the pseudonym of Mark Rutherford and all presented as posthumously edited by Rutherford's friend Reuben Shapcott – I propose to discuss only *The Revolution in Tanner's Lane* (1887) and *Clara Hopgood* (1896). The former is in some respects a puzzling work. It seems to be two novels loosely put together under a title appropriate only to the second. The first is the story of Zachariah Coleman, the evangelical radical, and his unsympathetic wife, set in the period immediately after the Napoleonic wars when the urban working classes suffered appalling hardships and a jittery government sent its spies to watch and frequently to apprehend those who were trying to organize demonstrations in favour of reform. The second part is set in Cowfold (White's native Bedford) and tells the story of the coarse and self-important minister of Tanner's Lane Chapel, the Reverend John Broad, and his family and their relations with the more humane and sensitive Allen family whose intelligent and sympathetic son marries the Broads' loving but totally empty-headed daughter. The ostensible link between the two parts is that the Allens had been friends of Zachariah Coleman (who now lives in London, a second time a widower, with his attractive daughter by his second wife) and Coleman and his daughter play a minor part in the plot. The 'Revolution' of the title refers to changes in ways of thinking and feeling about religion and ethics which take place not only in Tanner's Lane Chapel but in the atmosphere of Cowfold as a whole when the coarse Broad succeeds the 'lean and fervid' Reverend James Harden and is in turn succeeded at the end of the novel by a very modern young man from the University of London. Yet the title makes little sense if it refers only to religious changes in

Cowfold. We remember that Zachariah's story is not only the story of an active radical but that of a devout Calvinist whose religious ideas are tested and stretched by his various experiences. Tanner's Lane Chapel, as a traditionally English centre of nonconformist worship, clearly stands for something larger than itself: the revolution in Tanner's Lane must refer to social and religious problems and changes that are focused now on the history of Zachariah, now on the families of Cowfold. Nearly every significant character in the novel is forced sooner or later to reconsider the values by which he has lived or imagines he has lived. Is this what White meant by the revolution?

It is difficult to say. Indeed, if we read the novel as we read any other Victorian novel we are liable to get bewildered. The scale of the action keeps shifting. At one moment we get a detailed account of an incident or of a character's mood, at another we are rushed across time and space at bewildering speed. Zachariah's second marriage, the birth of his daughter, and the death of his second wife, are told in five lines. We recognize certain situations, certain sentiments, certain crises of mood and opinion, from the author's other works as belonging to his own life. He frequently intervenes with overt moralizing. At the same time, in the first part of the novel, the insistent social note, the vivid account of the futile meetings of the Friends of the People, and the assassination of its drunken and treacherous secretary, the equally vivid picture of the ill-fated march of the Blanketeers from Manchester to present a petition to the Government, the accounts of Zachariah's desperate flight from London to

Manchester and more desperate flight from Manchester to Liverpool and his stay in the Workhouse in the latter city – all this bears little relation to White's own personal life and reads like a novel of social protest. Yet *The Revolution in Tanner's Lane* is not a novel of social protest. It is a novel of ethical exploration in which, as in *Mark Rutherford's Deliverance*, the author uses social material to help focus its ethical points. And its critical concerns are with human relationships and with the ethical and psychological problems which they illuminate.

In the opening chapter Zachariah is watching Louis XVIII being cheered by crowds in London on his ceremonial visit there after the defeat of Napoleon at the Battle of Leipzig and the subsequent restoration of the Bourbons. White breaks into the narrative with a comment in his own person:

> There was a great crowd in the street when he came out of the hotel, and immense applause; the mob crying out, 'God bless your Majesty!' as if they owed him all they had, and even their lives. It was very touching, people thought at the time, and so it was. Is there anything more touching than the waste of human loyalty and love? As we read the history of the Highlands or a story of Jacobite loyalty such as that of Cooper's Admiral Bluewater, dear to boys, we sadden that destiny should decree that in a world in which piety is not too plentiful it should run so pitifully to waste, and that men and women should weep hot tears and break their hearts over bran-stuffing and wax.

'Is there anything more touching than the waste of human loyalty and love?' It is the kind of question that might have been posed by George Eliot (with whom, incidentally, White had considerable affinity and who appears in *The Autobiography of Mark Rutherford* as Theresa). But it is more than a moral generalization: it is a warning of the ethical watchfulness of the author and an indication of the way in which the novel should be read. For the novel is largely about human loyalty and love, sometimes wasted, sometimes not. No concessions at all are made to the normal demands of the novel form. White did not in fact work through the normal nineteenth-century novel form, as did all the other nineteenth-century novelists (Mrs Humphrey Ward, for example, in *Robert Elsmere*) who discussed either the social problem or the crisis of faith. There is no romantic plot, no conventional happy (or unhappy) ending, and, most of all, marriage, like other kinds of human relationship, is presented in order to help the author explore human needs, human responses, human self-delusions, and a variety of other moral and psychological problems. Once the proper kind of exploration has been achieved, one of the partners becomes unnecessary and is liable to be killed off suddenly. Characters are introduced and dismissed in order to light up some particular facet of the author's thought. Thus they can appear unexpectedly and be dismissed peremptorily. The form and meaning of the novel lies in what might be called its ethical texture. White has managed somehow to fuse the personal meditation, the social documentary, the moral fable, the Platonic dialogue, and the ethico-psychological case history into a literary form peculiarly appropriate to its purpose. Such a form provides no model for anybody else; it is too blatantly, and sometimes awkwardly, designed for a personal need. Yet it comes off. The awkwardness does not lessen the appropriateness of the form: it is part of the author's honesty. All this makes it difficult to discuss a Mark Rutherford novel, because the vocabulary we use in discussing novels was developed with reference to a different sort of novel form.

The first movement of the novel involves bringing in the lively young radical officer Major Maitland as a means of illuminating the unsatisfactory relationship between Zachariah and his wife and also as a means of involving Zachariah with the cultured French shoemaker Jean Caillaud and his attractive daughter Pauline. In the resulting interaction of characters, Zachariah's social and religious views are tested and disturbed. All of Matthew Arnold's concern about the relation of the religious to the aesthetic (and the place of both in human experience) is given disturbingly concrete embodiment in a remarkable scene in which Pauline, with deliberate consciousness of her bodily attractiveness, dances for Zachariah. The Caillauds are liberal-minded Deists, and their culture challenges Zachariah's calvinistic narrowness. Yet the debate between them is not one between enlightenment and reaction. The dialectic is subtle, worked out partly by argument and partly by the changing ways in which the characters relate to each other. When Zachariah quotes the biblical text 'I form the light and create darkness: I make peace and create evil; I the Lord do all these things' he is illustrating the strength of Calvinism, which does not shrink from any of the horrors of the world but insists that an all-powerful God is responsible for everything, both good and bad: White had none of the sentimental optimism of some kinds of 'liberal' religious thinkers. And when Pauline quotes the text back at him to defend her dancing, a new dimension is added to the argument. And all the time the social problem, the 'condition of England question', is being vividly and bitterly presented.

Unsatisfactory marriages – and there are many of them in White's novels – play an important part in testing values. Zachariah's cold and ungenerous wife is not a villain, but a compassionate study of the inability to *relate*, while, in the second part of the novel, George Allen's growing discontent with his stupid but loving wife Priscilla reminds us (as the relation between M'Kay and his wife does in *Mark Rutherford's Deliverance*) of the ethical complexities involved in human relationships – for in both cases the wife is justified and the husband obtains a new understanding when the wife suffers and then dies. The perfunctory use of death in the novels (Jean Caillaud is hanged) is not really perfunctory. There is a kind of ballet-like movement between people, some of whom appear on the stage to participate in a movement and disappear when that movement is over. Similarly, in *The Autobiography of Mark Rutherford* the hero rejects, with the reader's strong approval, the unintellectual Ellen to whom he has rashly become engaged, but in the *Deliverance*, after Ellen has been married to someone else and widowed and the hero has been through a great deal, they meet again in a scene that is both gentle and powerful and eventually marry and find a deep happiness in marriage.

It would take more than one lecture to trace out in detail the developing meanings of *The Revolution in Tanner's Lane*. All I can do now is to suggest where to look for its strengths and what sort of strengths are to be found. Perhaps the best way of concluding my remarks about the novel is to quote a few of the ethical pointers which the author inserted into it at intervals.

> He was not a ranter or revivalist, but what was called a moderate Calvinist; that is to say, he held to Calvinism as his undoubted creed, but when it came to the push in actual practice he modified it. In this respect he was inconsistent; but who is there who is not? His theology probably had no more gaps in it than that of the latest and most enlightened preacher who denies miracles and affirms the Universal Benevolence.

This was à propos of Zachariah's calvinist faith. A few pages further on we come across the familiar stoic theme, but in a new guise. Zachariah has discovered after three months of marriage that there is no real love between him and his wife and there can be no joy in the marriage relationship:

> Only thirty years old, and only three months a husband, he had already learned renunciation. There was to be no joy in life? Then he would be satisfied if it were tolerable, and he strove to dismiss all his dreams and do his best with what lay before him. Oh my hero! Perhaps somewhere or other – let us hope it is true a book is kept in which human worth is duly appraised, and in that book, if such a volume there be, we shall find that the divinest heroism is not that of the man who, holding life cheap, puts his

> back against a wall, and is shot by Government soldiers, assured that he will live ever afterwards as a martyr and saint: a diviner heroism is that of the poor printer, who, in dingy, smoky Rosoman Street, Clerkenwell, with forty years before him, determined to live through them, as far as he could, without a murmur, although there was to be no pleasure in them. A diviner heroism is this, but divinest of all, is that of him who can in these days do what Zachariah did, and without Zachariah's faith.

It is thus the George Eliot type, who holds God and Immortality to be unreal but who holds fast by Duty, that receives, or seems to receive, Hale White's highest praise. But again, we must test every remark of this kind by the action which surrounds it. The unexpected is always happening, and sometimes sheds new light on cultural patterns of the nineteenth century. The calvinist radical who had never been to a theatre before he met Major Maitland, who was disturbed and shocked at the idea of dancing, nevertheless became an enthusiast for Byron:

> The relationship between himself and his wife during those two years had become, not openly hostile, it is true, but it was neutral. Long ago he had given up the habit of talking to her about politics, the thing which lay nearest to his heart just then. The pumping effect of bringing out a single sentence in her presence on any abstract topic was incredible, and so he learned at last to come home, though his heart and mind were full to bursting, and say nothing more to her than that he had seen her friend Mrs Sykes, or bought his tea at a different shop. On the other hand, the revolutionary literature of the time, and more particularly Byron, increasingly interested him. The very

> wildness and remoteness of Byron's romance was just what suited him. It is all very well for the happy and well-to-do to talk scornfully of poetic sentimentality. Those to whom a natural outlet for their affection is denied know better. They instinctively turn to books which are the farthest removed from commonplace and are in a sense unreal. Not to the prosperous man, a dweller in beautiful scenery, well married to an intelligent wife, is Byron precious, but to the poor wretch, say some City clerk, with an aspiration beyond his desk, who has two rooms in Camberwell; . . .

It is all very well for Housman to exclaim rhetorically

> The troubles of our proud and angry dust
> Are from eternity, and shall not fail.
> Bear them we can, and if we can we must.

But what exactly are those sorrows and in what sense will they not fail? And how do we bear them? What comforts are available (in addition to Housman's symbolic ale) and where are they to be found? Hale White is never content to take a stance: his novels keep undermining stances, yet a careful reading yields in the end a firm pattern. This is especially true in his last novel, *Clara Hopgood*, published in 1896. This novel goes beyond Hardy's *Tess* (published five years before) in making a frontal attack on Victorian sexual prejudices. One of the principal characters, an intelligent and cultured girl, falls in love with and gets engaged to a wholly respectable and entirely eligible young man, and when they have to seek refuge alone together for two hours in a barn in a thunderstorm they surrender to sexual passion and she becomes pregnant. Immediately afterwards she realizes that she does not love him and insists on breaking off the engagement. He is hurt and outraged and pleads with her to marry him after all; but she is adamant. She deliberately chooses not to be 'made an honest woman of' rather than marry someone whom she has discovered she neither loves nor admires. The young man's subsequent behaviour bears out her opinion of him, though it takes a long time to emerge.

But Madge Hopgood's determination to bear her child unmarried rather than marry a man she had ceased to love and respect is not the central theme of the novel. The title, after all, is the name of Madge's elder sister Clara. The difference in character between the two girls is admirably projected in a dialogue between them over a game of chess in Chapter III – Madge is the more intuitive in making initial judgements, and only reflects afterwards; Clara deliberates more before coming to any conclusion – and it looks at first as though this is to be an engaging but conventional novel of two lively girls seeking husbands in an English provincial town. But the religious and ethical theme emerges early, if at first indirectly. The girls' widowed mother is religious in a highly personal way; she had no use for formal religion or for churchgoing; she was tolerant and liberal-minded. The girls were both sent for a time to a school in Weimar where they lived with a German lady who introduced them 'to the great German classics'. Madge had previously spent a brief time at a boarding-school in Brighton, but was asked to leave when it was discovered that she had never been christened and did not profess any particular brand of Christianity.

Madge's refusal to marry her fiancé and preference for bearing her baby by him out of wedlock totally disrupts the family life. They have to leave the provincial town where they have lived and seek lodgings in London. There they meet unkindness and prejudice, but also kindness and understanding – the latter not always from the most cultured, but notably from Mrs Caffyn, a morally heroic figure who nevertheless fits into no accepted social or moral pattern of the period. Clara gets a job to support the three of them. Mrs Hopgood suddenly catches a cold which leads to a fever and she dies: the two girls and Madge's baby are on their own. But they have friends, and in particular they become friends with one Baruch Cohen, whose relation to his ancestral Judaism is rather like that of William Hale White to his ancestral Christianity. Cohen (like White) is a student of Spinoza. He is an older man, a widower, with a grown-up son. He and Clara are mutually attracted; but in a remarkable scene she withdraws when he is on the point of leading the conversation to a proposal of marriage – withdraws at the very moment when she sees in her mind's eye a picture of future domesticity, conjugal love, emotional security. And she arranges that Madge and Baruch should be thrown together. Only an independent, philosophical moralist like Baruch would be able to defy popular prejudice and marry a girl who already had an illegitimate child. (This point is not made openly, but it is clearly the motive for Clara's heroic action.) Clara goes off to Italy to work for the Italian Risorgimento, presumably as a spy, and dies there within two years.

Clara Hopgood has often been read as a confused and incompetent novel; but I agree with Irvin Stock that it 'represents in many ways the highest development of [White's] genius'. In presenting the conflicting claims of the life of spontaneity and of reflection White is not pitting the good against the bad but exploring a deep ambiguity within himself. Everything in the novel – the dialogue, the social setting, the characters and their reactions on each other – is related to the exploration of this ambiguity. Is spontaneity just emotional selfishness and is deliberation cold calculation? The answer in each case is both yes and no; everything depends on circumstances, situations, individuals. But in the end renunciation is seen (yet not quite in Christian terms) as the highest ethical good – if it is renunciation for others' happiness. Early in the novel Clara tells her sister's fiancé, Frank, a story of a widower with an only daughter whom he dearly loved. The daughter suffered from periodical fits of total mental abstraction, and during one of those fits unconsciously appropriated a handkerchief when out shopping with her father and put it in her handbag. Her father discovered this and for his daughter's sake claimed, when the theft was discovered, that he had stolen the handkerchief. He was prosecuted and imprisoned. The daughter to the end of her life had no idea that she herself had taken the handkerchief: she recovered from her mental trouble and married happily. She believed that her father had taken the handkerchief by mistake. Only after the death of all the parties concerned was a statement of the father's opened, revealing the truth.

The father's lie saved his daughter's sanity and happiness. Was it justified? The two sisters argue the point. A lie is surely justified, says Madge, to save someone you love. 'Is a contemptible little two-foot measuring-tape to be applied to such an action as that?' But Clara is not so sure. 'We are always trying to transcend the rule by some special pleading, and often in virtue of some fancied superiority. Generally speaking, the attempt is fatal.' Frank does not know what position to take up.

Irving Stock, in his admirable book[1] on William Hale White, has shown the profound significance of this incident for the novel as a whole. This is how the novel ends:

> 'Father,' said a younger Clara to Baruch some ten years later as she sat on his knee, 'I had an Aunt Clara once, hadn't I?'
>
> 'Yes, my child.'
>
> 'Didn't she go to Italy and die there?'
>
> 'Yes.'
>
> 'Why did she go?'
>
> 'Because she wanted to free the poor people of Italy who were slaves.'

I can do no better than quote Dr Stock's comment:

> Many have found the last page of the novel either pointless or a mere 'realistic' trailing off. In fact, it is a final neces-

[1] Irving Stock: *William Hale White (Mark Rutherford), A Critical Study*. London, 1956.

sary step in the development of the central theme. It is also the saddest of Hale White's endings. That story Clara had told of the father who goes to his grave misunderstood by his beloved daughter for whom he has sacrificed himself has now become her own. For she lies in the earth, and Baruch, whom she loved, calmly repeats that error behind which her love and her sacrifice will now be concealed for ever. The obliteration of the act which most completely expressed her nature, and might well have crowned her life with glory, is a second death, and it is a kind of death which, for Hale White, has always added a special horror to the first. To be forgotten or misjudged after death – a despairing fear of this recurs often in his work. That he visits it upon Clara, however, is a sort of final honour. It is as though only the most terrible, the most total, of earthly martyrdoms would be commensurate with the spiritual majesty to which she has been lifted by her sacrifice.

In *The Autobiography of Mark Rutherford* White makes the point that the Christian doctrine of the Atonement, whatever its other theological claims may be, at least corresponds to a real truth – in real life people are always paying the penalty for others; people really are 'saved from penalties because another pays the penalty'. Madge chooses the wrong fiancé, gets herself pregnant by him before she realizes her mistake and breaks off the engagement, plunges her mother and sister into confusion and distress, forces her sister to go out to work, and is indirectly responsible for her mother's death. And in the end Clara pays. Yet it is not as ethically simple as that, for Baruch Cohen, whom Clara loved and whom Madge marries, is a symbolic character of great complexity and the relation of each of the girls to him has other meanings too. But it would take me too far afield to explore these.

I wanted to end my discussion of 'some late Victorian attitudes' with William Hale White partly because he is a remarkable writer who is too little read, partly because he spells out kinds of social and religious concern in an intimate and detailed way that no other writer of the time can match, partly because in his last novel he gives a remarkable new psychological and ethical twist to an old Christian doctrine. But it is dangerous to try and simplify what White has projected so complexly and so cunningly yet with a remarkable directness of style. The social historian, the historian of ideas and the literary critic might well get together to discover the best way of defining the many claims White's novels have on our attention. They are not easy to describe because they are so unlike other novels. This makes it all the more necessary that they should be not merely written about, but read.

Index

Index